# Calculations

6

PUBLISHED BY THE PRESS SYNDICATE OF THE UNIVERSITY OF CAMBRIDGE
The Pitt Building, Trumpington Street, Cambridge, United Kingdom

CAMBRIDGE UNIVERSITY PRESS
The Edinburgh Building, Cambridge CB2 2RU, UK
40 West 20th Street, New York, NY 10011-4211, USA
10 Stamford Road, Oakleigh, VIC 3166, Australia
Ruiz de Alarcón 13, 28014 Madrid, Spain
Dock House, The Waterfront, Cape Town 8001, South Africa

http://www.cambridge.org

First published 2001

Printed in the United Kingdom at the University Press, Cambridge

*Typefaces* Frutiger, Helvetica, Minion, Swift *System* QuarkXPress®4.03

*A catalogue record for this book is available from the British Library*

ISBN 0 521 78491 3 paperback

Text illustration Gary Rees

**General editors** for Cambridge Mathematics Direct
Sandy Cowling, Jane Crowden, Andrew King, Jeanette Mumford

**Writing team** for *Calculations 6*
Anne Barber, Salliann Coleman, Sandy Cowling, Zubeida Dasgupta, Claire Grigson, Gill Hatch,
Jeanette Mumford, Gary Murrell, Mary Nathan, Marian Reynolds, Kate Sharpe, Allison Toogood, Fay Turner

The writers and publishers would like to thank the many schools and
individuals who trialled lessons for Cambridge Mathematics Direct.

## Abbreviations and symbols

IP Interactive picture

CM Copymaster

A is practice work

B develops ideas

C is extension work

★ if needed, helps with work in A

A red margin indicates that activities are teacher-led.

A green margin indicates that activities are independent.

# Contents

# The relationship between addition and subtraction

| Key idea | You can rearrange numbers in a number sentence to create other number sentences. |
|----------|----------------------------------------------------------------------------------|

**★1** | **36 + 21 = 57**

Use this to help you answer these questions.

**a** 21 + 36 = ☐     **b** 57 − 21 = ☐     **c** 57 − 36 = ☐

**★2** | **25 + 54 = 79**

Use the numbers from this number sentence to write 3 other number facts.

**A1** | **3.6 + 2.8 = 6.4**

Use this to help you answer these questions.

**a** 2.8 + 3.6 = ☐     **b** 6.4 − 2.8 = ☐     **c** 6.4 − 3.6 = ☐

**A2** | **1.9 + 5.7 = 7.6**

Use the numbers from this number sentence to write 3 other number facts.

**A3** | **473 + 241 = 714**

Use this to help you answer these questions.

**a** 473 + 245 = ☐     **b** 470 + 241 = ☐

**c** 714 − 242 = ☐     **d** 712 − 473 = ☐

**A4** | You need a calculator.

Subtraction is the inverse of addition.

Use this to check your answers to A3 with a calculator.

Write what you do to check.

Use the facts given to find the answers.

**B1**   **4563 + 2654 = 7217**

a  7215 − 2654      b  4570 + 2654      c  7217 − 4555

**B2**   **6532 − 1756 = 4776**

a  6530 − 1756      b  4770 + 1756      c  6535 − 1756

**B3**   **9.99 − 3.82 = 6.17**

a  10.00 − 3.85      b  6.13 + 3.85      c  10.01 − 6.19

**B4**   You need a calculator.

Subtraction is the inverse of addition.

Use this to check your answers to B1, B2 and B3 with a calculator.

Write what you do to check.

**C1**   a  5192 + 2783 = ☐

b  Make up 3 related addition and subtraction problems that use slightly different numbers.

c  Work out the answers to your questions.

**C2**   Repeat C1 for  6.73 − 4.48 = ☐

| **Key idea** | You can rearrange numbers in a number sentence to create other number sentences. |
|---|---|

# Using rounding to estimate an answer

> **Key idea** | You can use rounding to estimate an answer.

★1

Dennis's log book

| Day | Litres |
|---|---|
| Monday | 48 |
| Tuesday | 57 |
| Wednesday | 32 |
| Thursday | 38 |
| Friday | 20 |

a Round each amount to the nearest 10 litres.

b Use your answers to a to work out roughly how much fuel he used in the week.

This chart shows how far Dennis drove making his deliveries each day last week.

Dennis's log book

| Day | Kilometres |
|---|---|
| Monday | 388 |
| Tuesday | 421 |
| Wednesday | 294 |
| Thursday | 323 |
| Friday | 162 |

A1  a How far did Dennis drive altogether on Wednesday and Thursday?

b How far did he drive on Monday and Tuesday?

> Use a near doubles method.

A2  a Round each distance to the nearest 100 km.

b Use your answers to a to work out approximately how far Dennis drove during the week.

A3  Repeat A2, but this time round each distance to the nearest 10 km.

**B1** Here are 2 receipts from the market.
The totals are illegible.

| Greg's groceries | |
|---|---|
| Bread | 0.65 |
| Jam | 2.07 |
| Beans | 0.32 |
| Crackers | 0.98 |
| Chocolate | 0.28 |
| Soap | 0.43 |
| Biscuits | 0.62 |
| Raisins | 1.00 |
| Mustard | 0.58 |
| Gravy | 0.79 |
| Lollipop | 0.16 |
| Toothpaste | 1.89 |
| TOTAL | xxxx |

| Homewares | |
|---|---|
| CD | 10.98 |
| Video | 14.25 |
| Magazine | 3.99 |
| Book | 8.75 |
| Hairbrush | 7.30 |
| White paint | 4.99 |
| Paint brushes | 6.55 |
| Biscuit box | 9.15 |
| Vase | 11.75 |
| Bar-b-q | 24.99 |
| TOTAL | xxxxx |

**a** Estimate the total for each receipt.

**b** Did you round to the nearest 10p or £1 for both receipts or did you round differently for each?

Explain the reasons for your decision.

*You can use a calculator.*

**B2** Find the actual totals and see how close your estimates were.

| Month | Kilometres | Month | Kilometres |
|---|---|---|---|
| January | 6280 | July | 1342 |
| February | 4345 | August | 2902 |
| March | 5916 | September | 4874 |
| April | 6107 | October | 5003 |
| May | 3598 | November | 6943 |
| June | 5591 | December | 3476 |

*Use mental methods and jottings.*

**C1** **a** How far did Dennis drive altogether in September and October?

**b** How far did he drive in March and April?

**C2** **a** Round each distance to the nearest 1000 km to estimate how far Dennis drove in one year.

**b** Total the actual distances, then find the difference between this distance and your estimate.

**C3** Repeat C2, this time rounding to the nearest 100 km.

How much closer to the actual distance is this estimate than the previous one?

| Key idea | You can use rounding to estimate an answer. |
|---|---|

# AS1.3  Checking answers

| Key idea | You can use different calculations to check answers. |
|---|---|

**A1**  Work mentally to find the missing numbers.
Show your method.

**a**  3400 + 6700 = ☐    **b**  4800 + 5900 = ☐

**c**  8300 − 3600 = ☐    **d**  6500 − 2800 = ☐

**e**  5700 − ☐ = 1800    **f**  2700 + ☐ = 6300

**g**  1900 + ☐ = 3700    **h**  ☐ − 7100 = 2600

**i**  ☐ − 2400 = 6800    **j**  ☐ + 6500 = 9200

**A2**  Use different mental methods to check your answers to A1.
Show your working.

**B1**  Hannah, Rachel, Tom and Robert are playing Superdarts.
Every turn they have 2 darts. Darts that land in the outer ring score double.

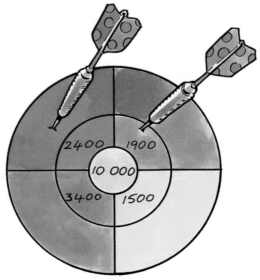

score :  1900 + (2 × 2400)
= 6700

**a**  If they score with both darts, what is the lowest score they could get?

**b**  What is the highest score they could get?

**c**  Hannah scored less than 5000. One of her darts was double 1500.
The other one landed on the board.

What did her second dart score?

**d**  Hannah and Rachel both threw a double. Rachel's double was 800 more than Hannah's.

What doubles did they throw?

**B2**  Use different mental methods to check your answers to B1.

Show your working.

**C1**  **a**  Draw your own dartboard.

**b**  Number your dartboard so that it is possible, with both darts landing on the board, to score all the multiples of 1000 between 2000 and 10 000.

Your numbers must be 4-digit multiples of 100.

Show how it is possible to make the scores using your board.

**c**  What is the lowest total you could make on your board?

**d**  What is the highest total you could make on your board?

**e**  Check your answers.

**C2**  Repeat C1, this time with 3-digit multiples of 100, so that it is possible to score all the multiples of 100 between 1200 and 2000.

| Key idea | You can use different calculations to check answers. |
|---|---|

# AS1.4 Adding 4-digit numbers mentally

| Key idea | To add 4-digit numbers mentally, start with the thousands. |
|---|---|

**A1** Add these numbers mentally. Use columns to help you add the parts.

a
```
   3 2 7 2
 + 4 3 2 9
```

b
```
   5 1 2 5
 + 3 4 6 2
```

c
```
   6 3 8 4
 + 3 5 6 9
```

d   6217 + 1645

e   4835 + 1245

f   2574 + 8369

This table shows the number of cans of drinks sold at seaside kiosks during a week in August.

| | Monday | Tuesday | Wednesday | Thursday | Friday | Saturday | Sunday |
|---|---|---|---|---|---|---|---|
| Cola | 988 | 876 | 1005 | 1456 | 3457 | 2543 | 2165 |
| Orangeade | 1258 | 934 | 754 | 1052 | 1008 | 1804 | 2054 |
| Lemonade | 745 | 1987 | 2365 | 678 | 3677 | 3402 | 3567 |

**B1** a   How many cans of orangeade and cola were sold on Monday?

b   How many were sold on Wednesday?

**B2** How many cans were sold at the weekend?

a

b

c

**B3** How many cans were sold in total on Wednesday?

**B4** How many cans of cola were sold altogether from Wednesday to Friday?

**C1** Calculate how many cans were sold during the whole week.

a

b

c

**C2** Check your answers to C1.

## AS1.5 Carrying

| Key idea | Begin with the digit with the smallest value when using short column addition. |
|---|---|

**★1** Use short column addition for these.

a
```
  5 3 6
+ 2 1 7
```

b
```
  4 1 9
+ 2 5 6
```

c
```
  3 4 2
+ 5 2 9
```

d
```
  7 4 2
+ 1 7 4
```

e
```
  4 8 1
+ 2 6 5
```

f
```
  3 5 7
+ 2 6 8
```

**A1** You need a partner, a calculator and cards from CM 2.

Shuffle the cards and deal them so that you each have the same number of cards.

a Use short column addition to find the total of your own numbers.

a Check your partner's work using a calculator to subtract back to the start number.

c Add your totals together.

£146.95

£29.99    £12.45    £9.59    £19.75

GAMES AND TOYS

**B1** How much would it cost to buy

a a netball and a football?    b a board game and a modelling kit?

c roller blades, a football and a board game?

d a modelling kit, a board game and roller blades?

Remember to check your calculations.

**B2** If you had £30 to spend on 2 items, what is the most you could spend?

**B3**   You need a calculator.

Use the calculator to check your answers to B1 and B2.

Show your working.

> 1600 g = 1.6 kg
> 800 g = 0.8 kg

**B4**   Write these weights in kg and add them up.

17 500 g          600 g          3400 g          74 500 g          2300 g          3000 g

**C1**

Here are the results of a field event triathlon:

|       | High jump | Long jump | Ball throw |
|-------|-----------|-----------|------------|
| Katie | 1 m 20 cm | 2 m 82 cm | 12 m 16 cm |
| Luke  | 98 cm     | 2 m 13 cm | 15 m 4 cm  |
| Sara  | 1 m 35 cm | 3 m 2 cm  | 10 m 87 cm |
| Scott | 1 m 12 cm | 3 m 55 cm | 13 m       |
| Emily | 1 m 9 cm  | 2 m 49 cm | 14 m 72 cm |

**a**   Scores are worked out by adding together the results from all 3 events.

Calculate each person's score.

**b**   In what order do the children finish?

| Key idea | Begin with the digit with the smallest value when using short column addition. |

# AS2.1 Using subtraction

| Key idea | You use a range of vocabulary to describe subtraction. |
|---|---|

**★1** Copy and complete these sets of related subtraction statements.

**a** $7 - 4 = 3$      $70 - 40 = \square$      $700 - 400 = \square$

**b** $50 - 10 = 40$      $500 - 100 = \square$      $5000 - 1000 = \square$

**c** $2200 - 1500 = 700$      $220 - 150 = \square$      $22 - 15 = \square$

**A1** Copy and complete these sets of related subtraction statements.

**a** $90 - 70 = 20$      $900 - 700 = \square$      $9000 - \square = 2000$

**b** $8 - 2 = 6$      $0.8 - 0.2 = \square$      $800 - \square = 600$

**c** $2.4 - 1.1 = 1.3$      $240 - \square = 130$      $24\,000 - 11\,000 = \square$

**d** $14\,000 - 3000 = 11\,000$      $140 - \square = 110$      $1.4 - 0.3 = \square$

**A2** Play 'Subdominoes'.

You need a partner and cards from CM 3.

**B1**  Give 2 related subtractions for each of these.

**a**  1100 − 600 = ☐        **b**  3.7 − 2.1 = ☐        **c**  18.4 − 12.8 = ☐

**B2**

24 300 supporters were at the football match this week.
That is 3700 more than there were last week.

How many were there last week?

**B3**  Find the missing numbers. Show your working.

**a**  960 − 340 = ☐        **b**  3500 − ☐ = 2400

**c**  ☐ − 4.8 = 0.9        **d**  650 − 285 = ☐

**B4**  **a**  How much less than 7.4 is 5.8?

**b**  Decrease 472 by 235.

**c**  3.8 add a number is 5.3. What is the number?

**d**  What is the difference between 8.2 and 2.7?

Make sure your stories are set in the real world.

**B5**  For each of the questions in B3 and B4, write a number story that matches the subtraction.

**C1**  Look at IP 10.

Write 6 subtraction problems based on IP 10.

| Key idea | You use a range of vocabulary to describe subtraction. |

IP 10

# AS2.2 Adding on in steps

**Key idea** | You can subtract by adding on in steps from the smaller number.

**A1** Use the counting up method to answer these questions.

**a**
$$\begin{array}{r} 5231 \\ -\ 3892 \\ \hline \end{array}$$

**b**
$$\begin{array}{r} 6185 \\ -\ 2346 \\ \hline \end{array}$$

**c**
$$\begin{array}{r} 8576 \\ -\ 4672 \\ \hline \end{array}$$

**d**
$$\begin{array}{r} 7264 \\ -\ 1698 \\ \hline \end{array}$$

**A2** Use the counting up method to answer these questions.

**a** 1300 – 296 = ☐

**b** 7832 – 2948 = ☐

**c** 4233 – 1133 = ☐

**d** 4762 – 2839 = ☐

**e** 12 103 – 9651 = ☐

**f** 25 601 – 14 801 = ☐

**A3** You need a calculator.

Use the calculator to check your answers to A1 and A2.

Record each calculation you do.

**C1** Find all the differences between pairs of these numbers.

**3781** **8418** **5642**

**4135** **6297**

## AS2.3 Subtracting decimals 1

| Key idea | You can subtract decimals in the same way as whole numbers. |
|---|---|

**A1** Lana sells rocks by length. These children have all bought some.

a What is the difference in length between the longest and the shortest piece of rock?

b How much shorter is Danny's rock than Esme's?

c How much longer is Lee's rock than Megan's?

Use a written counting up method.

d Esme eats 7.5 cm of her rock. How much is left?

e Lana started off with a 1 m stick of pink rock. How much is left?

**A2**

£8.99          £2.65          £6.72          £3.49

a Laura buys the CD. She pays with a £10 note.
How much change does she get?

b Jill buys the watch. She pays with a £5 note.
How much change does she get?

c How much more does the beach ball cost than the car?

d How much cheaper is the watch than the ball?

| Miss Hall | Becky | Sharon | Mr Cohen |
|-----------|-------|--------|----------|
| 3.47 kg | 6.8 kg | 13.2 kg | 8.94 kg |

a What is the difference in weight between the heaviest shopping and the lightest?

b How much more does Sharon's shopping weigh than Mr Cohen's?

c How much lighter is Miss Hall's shopping then Becky's?

Use a written counting up method.

d Sharon gives Miss Hall a lift home.
How much more does their shopping weigh than Becky's?

**B2** 5 children were comparing the lengths of their gardens.
They measured the lengths as:

  12.7 m    22.6 m    41.3 m    8.47 m    9.72 m

Find all the differences between the lengths.

**C1** Sarai has £10 in her purse when she goes shopping. She buys:

| £2.35 each | £3.99 | 38p each |
|------------|-------|----------|

How much money does she have left?

**C2** Alec Trician has a new spool of wire that is 120.8 m long.

a He uses 17.9 m on one job, 16.24 m on a second job and 20.05 m on a third job.
How much wire does he have left?

b He needs 135.5m of wire for his next job. How much must he get to have enough?

| Key idea | You can subtract decimals in the same way as whole numbers. |
|----------|-------------------------------------------------------------|

# AS2.4 Subtracting decimals 2

| Key idea | You can subtract decimals in the same way as whole numbers. |
|---|---|

**A1**  Copy and complete these subtractions.

a
```
  2 7 . 9
- 1 6 . 2
```

b
```
  3 4 . 6
- 1 8 . 4
```

c
```
  3 6 . 2
- 1 2 . 8
```

d
```
  3 . 8 7
- 2 . 2
```

e
```
  8 . 2 4
- 5 . 1 7
```

f
```
  7 . 2
- 3 . 4 8
```

**A2**  Mr Cohen bought fruit and vegetables.

He gave Stella £5.

How much change did he get?

72p   £1·12   £2·57

**A3**  Sharon bought fruit and vegetables.

She gave Stella £15.

How much change did she get?

£1·72   £2·68   £3·41   £3·25   £2·50

**B1** Write these as column subtractions and work them out.

a 72.5 – 33.8 = ☐    b 68.2 – 39.7 = ☐    c 50.4 – 31.8 = ☐

**B2** Take care how you line up these numbers!

a 47.8 – 3.5 = ☐    b 82.9 – 54 = ☐    c 63 – 24.6 = ☐

**B3** Find the difference between the lengths of these vehicles:

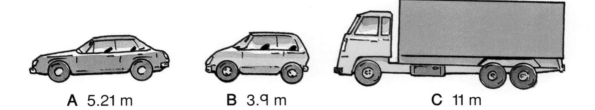

**A** 5.21 m          **B** 3.9 m          **C** 11 m

**B4** Write these as column subtractions and work them out.

a 8.6 – 2.22 = ☐    b 56.1 – 0.35 = ☐    c 7.64 – 2.8 = ☐

**C1** a You have £15. What 3 items will you buy from IP 10?

b How much money is left?

**C2** a You have £20.50. What 4 items will you buy from IP 10?

b How much money is left?

**C3** a You have £30.75. What 6 items will you buy from IP 10?

b How much money is left?

| Key idea | You can subtract decimals in the same way as whole numbers. |
| --- | --- |

# AS3.1  Adjusting by 0.1

| **Key idea** | When adding or subtracting decimals, it is sometimes easier to add or subtract a whole number, then adjust. |
|---|---|

Add or subtract the number in the circle to or from each of the numbers on the spokes.

**B1**

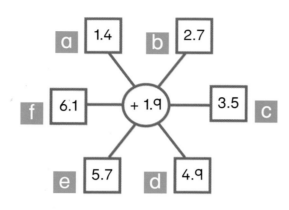
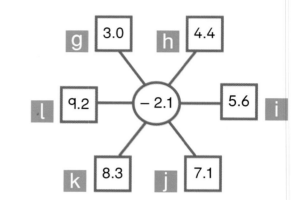

**B2**

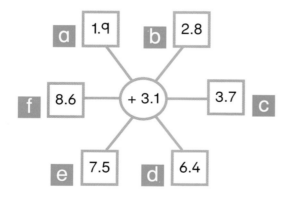
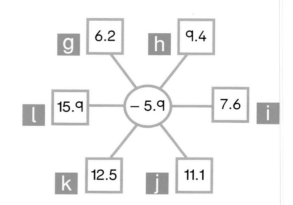

**B3**

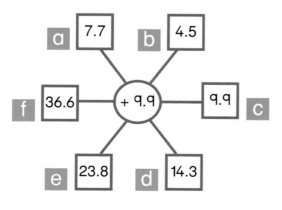
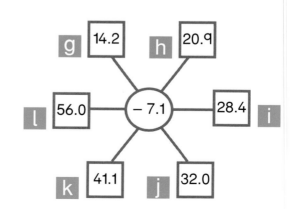

# AS3.2 Finding differences by counting up

| Key idea | Count up through the next multiple of 10, 100 or 1000 to find a difference between 4-digit numbers. |
|---|---|

**A1** Work out the answers in your head.

Count up from the smaller number to work out these differences. You can use jottings.

a 205 – 97  b 502 – 395  c 700 – 592  d 401 – 294

e 604 – 199  f 900 – 388  g 712 – 297  h 625 – 95

**A2** Work out these answers in your head by counting up. You can use jottings.

a 7000 – 2795  b 6000 – 3193  c 9000 – 6898  d 10 000 – 8899

e 6006 – 3788  f 8010 – 5375  g 4101 – 992  h 6375 – 5599

**B1** Work out the missing distance for each go-cart in the table.

**B2** Find the difference between these totals on the scoreboard:

a the two highest totals

b the highest and lowest totals

c the two highest odd totals

d the two lowest odd totals

| Name | Round 1 (metres) | Round 2 (metres) | Total (metres) |
|---|---|---|---|
| Troy | 1982 | a | 4800 |
| Titan | b | 2793 | 5079 |
| Tiger | 2827 | c | 5193 |
| Thad | d | 3946 | 4917 |
| Turk | 2897 | e | 5351 |
| Theo | f | 3828 | 5648 |

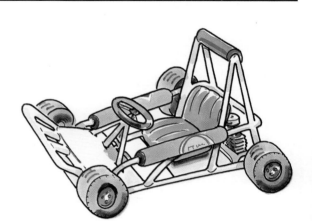

**B3** The overall winner was Triple wheel. Its total distance was 8214 m.

Find the difference between its total distance and each of the others.

**C1** 3756     6215     **8367**     7509

Find the difference between all the pairs of these numbers.

# AS3.3 Add and adjust

| Key idea | Add too much, and take off. |
|---|---|

**★1**  a  Choose 2 numbers from the bucket.

    b  Add them together.

789  598
670
973
884

Add too much,
then take off!

**★2**  Repeat ★1 for 2 more pairs of numbers.

**A1**  Choose 1 number from the bucket and
1 number from the box and add them together.

5692  6218
2775
4183  7039
3606

**A2**  Repeat A1 for 6 more calculations.

Add too much,
take off!

**A3**  Write these calculations vertically, then work out the answers.

a  1392 + 2886       b  7276 + 4798       c  3828 + 5026

d  2976 + 7296       e  5085 + 3678       f  8634 + 1289

g  6376 + 3575       h  4408 + 4840       i  7756 + 4008

**B1**  Write these calculations vertically and work them out.

a  58.36 + 27.84       b  33.54 + 29.62       c  45.14 + 36.96

d  127.9 + 12.79       e  52.87 + 334.6       f  23.75 + 68.75

g  67.58 + 0.71       h  116.7 + 0.35       i  235.5 + 0.67

**B2**  Do CM 9.

CM 9

**C1**

Copy each grid into your exercise book.

Add the rows across from left to right.

Add the columns downwards.

Write your answers in the empty spaces at the end of each row and column.

**a**

| 1678 | 825 | |
|------|------|--|
| 406 | 1776 | |
| | | |

Remember to fill in the bottom right-hand spaces.

**b**

| 2154 | 519 | |
|------|------|--|
| 3364 | 2781 | |
| | | |

**c**

| 5342 | 796 | |
|------|------|--|
| 2798 | 5976 | |
| | | |

**C2**

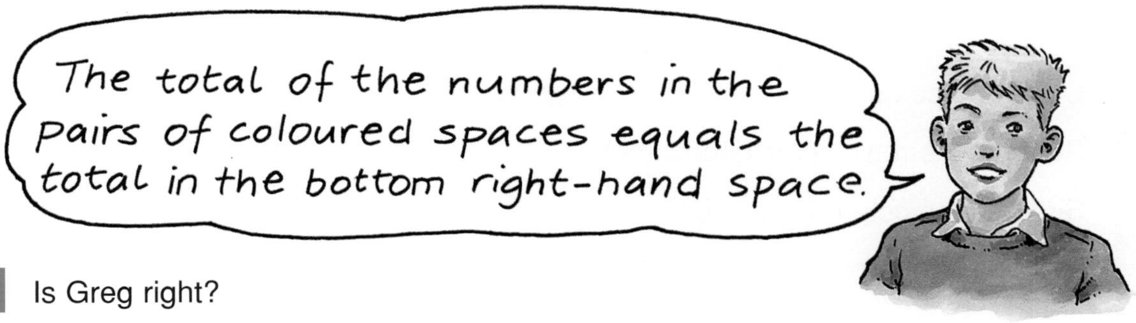

*The total of the numbers in the pairs of coloured spaces equals the total in the bottom right-hand space.*

**a** Is Greg right?

**b** Why?

| **Key idea** | Add too much, and take off. |
|---|---|

# AS3.4 Subtract and adjust

| **Key idea** | Take too much, add back |
| --- | --- |

**★1** Choose a different pair of numbers each time and make up 4 subtraction calculations.

Work out each answer.

**A1** Write these calculations vertically and work out the answers.

a  5185 – 2957      b  5613 – 4971      c  6147 – 1638

d  9927 – 3879      e  8047 – 5970      f  4253 – 1877

**A2** Choose a different pair of numbers each time.

Make up and solve 6 subtraction calculations.

**C1** Copy and complete these subtraction grids.

Subtract the rows across horizontally.

Subtract the columns vertically.

Write the differences in the empty spaces at the end of each row or column.

Check that the answer in the bottom right-hand square is correct for row 3 and column 3.

a

| 7575 | 5400 | |
| --- | --- | --- |
| 4287 | 3600 | |
| | | |

Take too much, add it back!

b

| 8142 | 6306 | |
| --- | --- | --- |
| 4944 | 3747 | |
| | | |

c

| 187.6 | 108.7 | |
| --- | --- | --- |
| 60.4 | 40.6 | |
| | | |

Add several numbers

| Key idea | Look for quick ways to add several numbers. |
|---|---|

**A1** Do CM 11.

**A2** Copy and complete.

a  $49 + 25 + 31 = \square$    b  $58 + 43 + 22 = \square$

c  $35 + 47 + 55 = \square$    d  $74 + 19 + 26 = \square$

**A3** Check your answers to A2. Record what you do.

**B1** Copy and complete.

a  $60 + 61 + 65 + 67 = \square$    b  $32 + 41 + 28 + 59 = \square$

c  $26 + 48 + 33 + 51 = \square$    d  $81 + 31 + 28 + 11 = \square$

**B2** Copy and complete.

a  $54 + \square + 46 = 134$    b  $21 + \square + 59 = 142$

c  $\square + 27 + 83 = 157$    d  $66 + \square + 64 = 196$

e  $26 + 31 + \square + 49 = 217$    f  $42 + \square + 51 + 38 = 189$

**B3** Copy and complete so that each side makes the same multiple of 10.

a  $37 + \square = 59 + \square$    b  $28 + \square = \square + 82$

c  $\square + 65 = \square + 46$    d  $\square + 29 = \square + 54$

**C1** Play 'Make multiples of 10'.

You need a 0–9 dice and 3 friends.

- Each draw a playing sheet like this:

$\square\square + \square\square + \square\square + \square\square =$

- Each player throws the dice in turn and all the players write the number in one of their boxes until all the boxes are full.
- Everyone whose total is a multiple of 10 scores a point. If no one gets a multiple of 10 then the player who is nearest to a multiple of 10 scores a point.
- Play 5 rounds and see who is the winner.

# AS4.2 Carrying with large numbers

| Key idea | Begin with the units when carrying across columns. |
| --- | --- |

**★1** Copy and complete these additions.

| a | | b | | c | | d | |
| --- | --- | --- | --- | --- | --- | --- | --- |
| | 2 4 7 | | 5 7 2 | | 6 7 4 | | 7 8 1 |
| + | 3 2 8 | + | 4 1 9 | + | 2 4 5 | + | 1 6 3 |

**A1** Copy and complete these additions.

| a | | b | | c | | d | |
| --- | --- | --- | --- | --- | --- | --- | --- |
| | 1 3 5 6 | | 2 7 3 9 | | 5 8 6 4 | | 6 2 4 7 |
| + | 2 4 9 8 | + | 5 1 8 6 | + | 3 4 2 8 | + | 4 2 3 8 |

**A2** Write these as column additions and find the answers.

a 35 178 + 4677 = ☐          b 8364 + 21 789 = ☐

c 2786 + 19 325 = ☐          d 24 623 + 17 196 = ☐

**B1** Sally and Mike worked out these additions. Which ones did they get right?

ⓐ 5186
+ 2746
8832

ⓑ 3456
+ 4717
7173

ⓒ 1894
+ 7231
9055

ⓓ 4587
+ 3643
8220

ⓔ 2345
+ 6098
8443

ⓕ 6432
+ 1693
8025

**B2** Work out the correct answers for any questions Sally and Mike got wrong.

**B3** Choose numbers from the box to answer these questions.

a Find 2 numbers that total 7713.

b Find 2 numbers that total 8026.

c Find 2 numbers that total 7038.

d What is the smallest total you can get by adding 2 of the numbers?

| | | |
|---|---|---|
| **4239** | | 5748 |
| 3128 | 6174 | |
| | | **2278** |
| **1965** | **3817** | **5073** |

e What is the highest total you can get by adding 2 of the numbers?

f What is the nearest you can get to 5000 by adding 2 of the numbers?

g What is the nearest you can get to 8000 by adding 2 of the numbers?

**C1** This machine adds 1369 to the input number.

Then the output goes back into the machine.

The machine stops when the output number is more than 10 000.

For an input of 6532 we get this chain:

$$6532 \xrightarrow{+1369} 7901 \xrightarrow{+1369} 9270 \xrightarrow{+1369} 10\ 639$$

a Work out the chain that starts with 5347.

b The machine cannot use negative numbers.

What 4-digit input number would give you the longest chain?

| **Key idea** | Begin with the units when carrying across columns. |
|---|---|

## AS4.3 Totalling several numbers

> **Key idea** | Make sure you place digits in the correct columns (units under units, tens under tens and so on).

**★1** Find the totals.

| a | | b | | c | |
|---|---|---|---|---|---|
| | 8 2 1 | | 5 1 2 3 | | 1 4 1 0 |
| | 9 5 | | 1 7 6 | | 3 9 7 |
| + | 3 6 | + | 4 9 | + | 1 5 3 |

These are the games and puzzles that contestants can take part in on the television show 'Adventure Game'.

4582 points

97 points

1765 points

247 points

576 points

3187 points

**A1** Rachel completed the star puzzle and the snake puzzle.

How many points did she score?

**A2** Ross completed the snake puzzle and the cave adventure.

How many points did he score?

**A3** Philip completed the snake puzzle, the treasure quest and the cat puzzle.

What was his final score?

**A4** Eleanor completed the car rally, the cave adventure, the star puzzle and the cat puzzle.

What was her final score?

**A5** Who was the winner?

**B1**

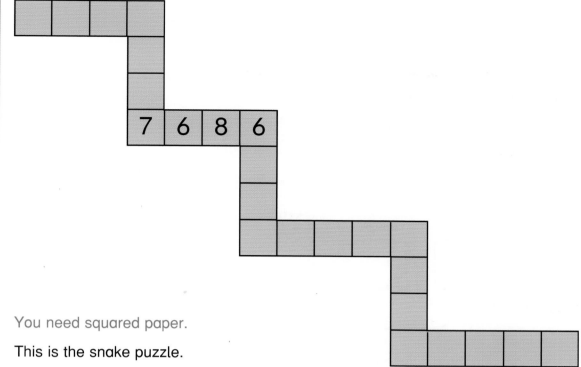

You need squared paper.

This is the snake puzzle.

Copy the snake.

Find the totals and fit them onto the snake so that the numbers follow on.

a   1976 + 153 + 49          b   39 + 585 + 6139 + 83

c   176 + 8123 + 95 + 821    d   3256 + 45 + 5126

e   12 243 + 676 + 36 963 + 6294    f   32 986 + 9251 + 24 582

**B2**

a   Take any 4-digit number, e.g. 4172.

b   Make 3 more numbers by moving the units digit to the front each time,
e.g. 2417, 7241, 1724

c   Add up the four numbers: 4172 + 2417 + 7241 + 1724 = 15 554

d   Try some different starting numbers.

How many different totals can you get?

e   Can you predict the total from the first number?

| Key idea | Make sure you place digits in the correct columns (units under units, tens under tens and so on). |
|---|---|

# AS4.4 Carrying and decimals

> **Key idea** | You can add decimals in the same way as whole numbers. You must line numbers up so that digits of the same value are under each other.

**★1** This number machine keeps adding on 3.4 until it gets to a whole number. Then it stops.

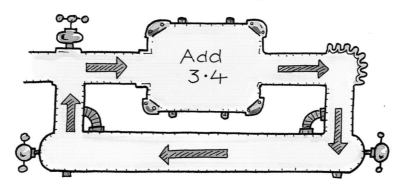

If 7.8 is put into the machine it goes 7.8 → 11.2 → 14.6 → 18

Because 18 is a whole number, the machine stops.

Work out when the machine stops when each of these numbers is put into it.

a 6.2     b 8.4     c 10.8     d 13.6     e 19.7

**A1** This number machine keeps adding on 5.38 until it makes a number greater than 50. Then it stops.

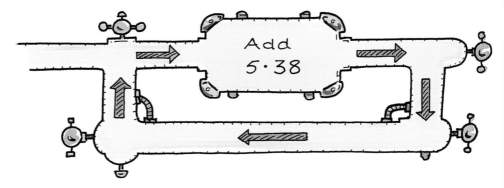

If 42.43 is put into the machine it goes 42.43 → 47.81 → 53.19

Because 53.19 is greater than 50, the machine stops.
Work out when the machine stops when each of these numbers is put into it.

a 37.29     b 29.63     c 25.02     d 47.56     e 72.92

**A2** A similar machine keeps adding 2.69.

Find out what it does to each of the numbers in A1.

**A3**

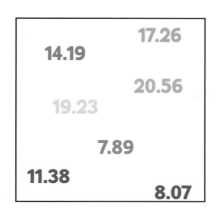

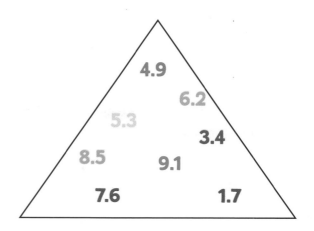

a   Add 2 numbers from the square and 1 number from the triangle.

b   Add 2 numbers from the triangle and 1 number from the square.

c   Add 2 numbers from the square and 2 numbers from the triangle.

d   What is the largest total that can be made from 2 numbers from the square and 2 numbers from the triangle?

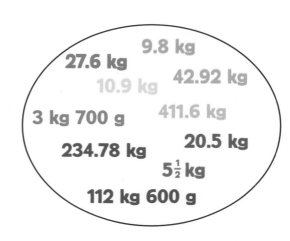

**B1**   Choose 2 masses to add up to give a total less than 10 kg. Find the total.

**B2**   Choose 2 masses to add up to give a total greater than 70 kg. Find the total.

**B3**   Choose 2 masses with a sum between 30 kg and 40 kg. Find their sum.

**B4**   Choose 3 masses with a sum a little less than 200 kg. Find their sum.

**B5**   Choose 2 masses that have a sum greater than 500 kg. Find their sum.

**B6**   Choose 3 masses that have a total near 350 kg. Find the total.

**B7**   Choose 5 masses. Find their sum.

**B8**   Find the total of the remaining 5 masses.

| **Key idea** | You can add decimals in the same way as whole numbers. You must line numbers up so that digits of the same value are under each other. |

# Choose your method 1

| Key idea | Choose the most appropriate method to solve a problem: mentally, pencil and paper or with a calculator. |
|---|---|

**B1** This number machine adds 273.

Sally put some numbers into it.
She only wrote down what came out.
Can you work out what numbers she put in?

| In | Out |
|---|---|
| a | 896 |
| b | 504 |
| c | 1298 |
| d | 2467 |

**B2** Sally put different numbers into this machine and was most surprised when the numbers that came out were the same as before.

What numbers did she put in this time?

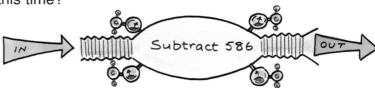

**B3** Zarif found some addition and subtraction machines in a cupboard.
They had lost their labels. Can you work out a label for each one?

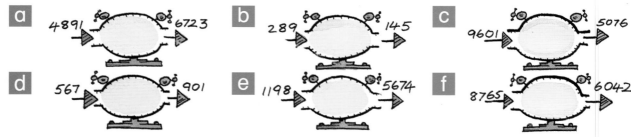

a 4891 → 6723

b 289 → 145

c 9601 → 5076

d 567 → 901

e 1198 → 5674

f 8765 → 6042

**C1** ▢ and △ represent the same numbers in both statements.

Can you work out what they are?

▢ + △ = 65          ▢ − △ = 35

**C2** Can you solve this one?

✩ + ▽ = 65          ✩ − ▽ = 11

**C3** Make up a puzzle like those in C1 and C2.

# AS5.3 Decomposition for decimals

| **Key idea** | You can subtract decimals in the same way as whole numbers. |
|---|---|

**★1**   Copy and complete.

**a**
```
  1 2 5 . 9
− 1 0 6 . 2
```

**b**
```
  3 1 8 . 7
− 1 5 3 . 6
```

**c**
```
  4 6 3 . 5
−   4 1 . 8
```

**A1**   Copy and complete.

**a**
```
  1 1 2 . 1
−   3 4 . 6
```

**b**
```
  6 9 2 . 4
− 1 2 7 . 7
```

**c**
```
  7 3 4
− 1 4 9 . 7
```

**A2**   Find the difference between the number in the centre and the number on the arm.

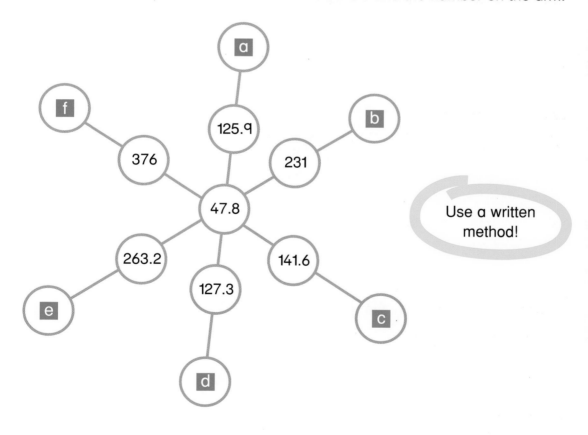

Use a written method!

Find the difference between the number in the centre and the number on the arm.

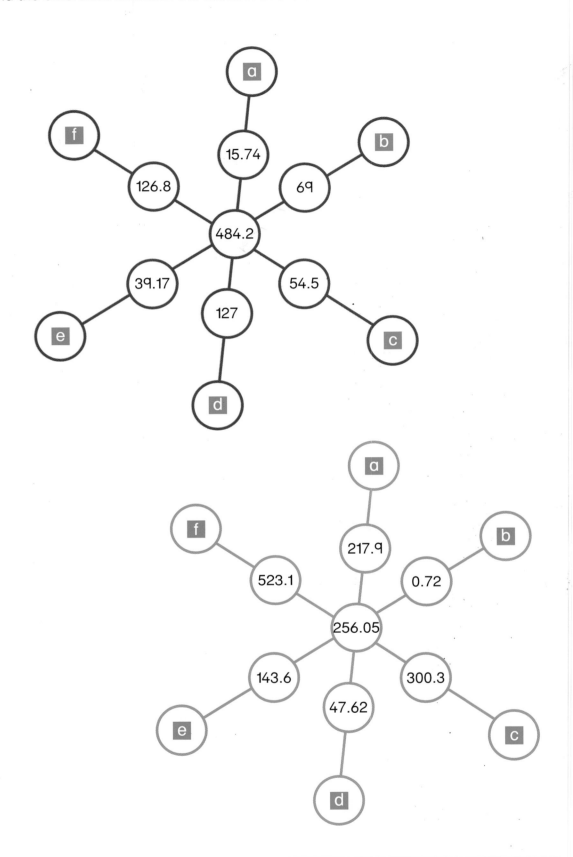

| Key idea | You can subtract decimals in the same way as whole numbers. |
| --- | --- |

# Make up to the next whole number

| Key idea | It is useful to know pairs of decimals that total 10. |

**B1** Solve these problems.

**3.67**

a  $3.67 + \square = 3.7$

b  What must be added to 1.45 to get to the next tenth?

c  What must be added to 5.83 to get to the next tenth?

**7.22**

d  $7.22 + \square = 7.3$

e  What must be added to 7.94 to get to the next tenth?

f  $3.06 + \square = 3.1$

g  Make up a problem like a for a friend to solve.

**1.45**

h  Make up a problem like b for a friend to solve.

Use an empty number line.

**B2** Solve these problems.

a  What must be added to 3.68 to get to the next whole number?

b  $4.81 + \square = 5$

**4.81**

c  What must be added to 6.34 to get to the next whole number?

d  $7.72 + \square = 8$

e  What must be added to 9.27 to get to the next whole number?

**9.27**

f  $3.05 + \square = 4$

g  Make up a problem like a for a friend to solve.

h  Make up a problem like b for a friend to solve.

**3.05**

# AS6.2 Adding and subtracting decimals mentally

| Key idea | Numbers less than 1 with 2 decimal places may be added or subtracted mentally in the same way as 2-digit numbers. |
|---|---|

**A1** Do CM 18.

**A2** Copy and complete.

a  0.9 – 0.4 = ☐   b  0.8 – 0.6 = ☐   c  0.76 – 0.02 = ☐

d  0.76 – 0.33 = ☐   e  0.59 – 0.26 = ☐   f  0.87 – 0.45 = ☐

**A3** Use addition to check your answers to A2.

**B1** Find the answers.

a  What is the difference between 0.45 and 0.83?

b  0.62 – 0.37 = ☐

c  How much bigger is 0.93 than 0.67?

d  Take 0.57 away from 0.92

e  £0.84 subtract £0.26

f  What is the difference between 0.28 kg and 0.82 kg?

g  0.78 m – 0.49 m

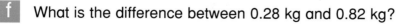

h  How much less is £0.17 than £0.43?

**B2** Check your answers to B1 using the inverse operation.

CM 18

**B3** Copy and complete.

a 0.52 + 0.29 = ☐    b 0.73 + 0.36 = ☐    c 0.84 + 0.42 = ☐

d 0.76 + 0.68 = ☐    e 0.92 + 0.75 = ☐    f 0.67 + 0.58 = ☐

**B4** Use the inverse operation to check your answers to B3.

**C1**

> Two numbers have a total of 0.83.
> One number is more than 0.5.
> The other ends with an even digit.

What could the 2 numbers be?

Find 5 pairs of possible answers.

**C2**

> Two numbers have a difference of 0.67.
> Both the numbers are less than 1.
> One number is more than 0.42.
> Both numbers end with odd digits.

What could the 2 numbers be?

Find 5 pairs of possible answers.

**C3** Make up 2 puzzles like Laura's and Kenny's.

Find 5 pairs of possible answers for each one.

| Key idea | Numbers less than 1 with 2 decimal places may be added or subtracted mentally in the same way as 2-digit numbers. |
|---|---|

# AS6.3 Adding and subtracting decimals in columns

| Key idea | Line up digits of the same value correctly to add or subtract in columns. |
|---|---|

**A1**

  **a** Choose 2 items and work out their total cost.

  **b** How much more did one of your items cost than the other?

**A2** Choose 3 other pairs of items from the shop.

For each pair, work out the total cost and the difference between their prices.

Give all your answers in pounds.

**A3** Karen has £4.35.

  **a** What 2 items could she buy? How much do they cost altogether?

  **b** How much money does she have left?

**B1**

  **a** Choose one amount from each of the money boxes below.

Find the total of the 2 amounts and the difference between them.

Give your answers in pounds.

  **b** Repeat for 3 more pairs of amounts.

**B2**   **a**   Choose one length from each of the sets below.

Find the total of the 2 lengths and the difference between them.

Give your answers in metres.

**b**   Repeat this for 3 more pairs of lengths.

**B3**   Choose one weight from each of the sets below.

**a**   Find the total of the 2 weights and the difference between them.

Give your answers in kg.

**b**   Repeat this for 3 more pairs.

**C1**

JAKE    JOSH    CLARE

Clare, Jake and Josh are triplets.

Mrs Brown is their mum. She buys them 3 birthday presents each.

**a**   Look at IP 13. Find 3 things that Mrs Brown might give Clare.

**b**   How much does she spend on Clare?

**c**   Repeat **a** and **b** for presents for Josh and Jake.

**d**   How much does Mrs Brown spend altogether?

| **Key idea** | Line up digits of the same value correctly to add or subtract in columns. |

# Choose your method 2

> | **Key idea** | Choose the most appropriate way of doing a calculation: mentally, using pencil and paper or a calculator. |

**A1**

**a** What is the total cost of the first 3 items?

**b** What is the total cost of the mug, the tissue paper and the magazine?

**c** What is the difference in the price between the magazine and the gift tags?

**d** What is the total cost of Laura's shopping?

**e** Laura has only brought £10 with her.

Choose what she could put back.

How much does her shopping cost now?

| Birthday card £1.38 |
| Gift tags 99p |
| Chocolate 62p |
| Mug £4.75 |
| Tissue paper £2.59 |
| Newspaper 37p |
| Magazine £3.68 |

*First choose how you will do each calculation.*

**A2** Use a rounding method to check your answers to A1.

**B1**

**a** What is the total weight of the potatoes and the mushrooms?

**b** How much heavier are the peaches than the sprouts?

**c** What is the difference in weight between the peaches and the tomatoes?

**d** How much does the shopping weigh altogether?

First choose how you will do each calculation.

**B2** Do CM 19.

**Key idea** | Choose the most appropriate way of doing a calculation: mentally, using pencil and paper or a calculator.

# Use your facts

| Key idea | $18 \times 23$ equals $23 \times 18$, but $18 \div 23$ does not equal $23 \div 18$. |
|---|---|

**B1** Using the numbers in each mobile, write 2 multiplication and 2 division facts.

**Example**

**a**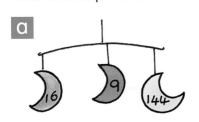

**b**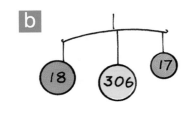

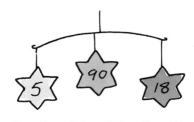

$5 \times 18 = 90 \qquad 90 \div 5 = 18$

$18 \times 5 = 90 \qquad 90 \div 18 = 5$

**c**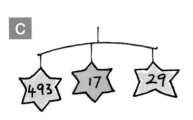

**d**

**B2** The number in each square is the product of the numbers in the circles on either side.

Copy and complete.

**a**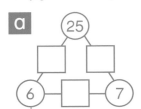

**b**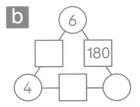

**c**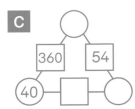

**d**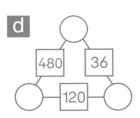

**e**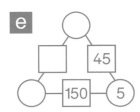

**f**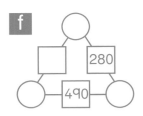

**B3** Copy and complete the table.

| Start with | 800 | 240 | 360 | 420 | 630 | 280 | 540 |
|---|---|---|---|---|---|---|---|
| Divide by | 20 | 30 | | 70 | | | 60 |
| Quotient | 40 | | 6 | | 21 | 7 | |

# Grouping and sharing

| Key idea | Sharing is better for dividing by small numbers. Grouping is better for dividing by larger numbers. |
|---|---|

**A1** Copy and complete.

a $102 \div 3 = \square$

b $172 \div 43 = \square$

c $384 \div 64 = \square$

d $532 \div 4 = \square$

e $259 \div 37 = \square$

f $276 \div 6 = \square$

Decide whether to use sharing or grouping.

**A2** Find the missing numbers.

a $76 \times \triangle = 532$

b $\triangle \times 6 = 282$

c $\triangle \times 3 = 189$

d $67 \times \triangle = 268$

e $3 \times \triangle = 219$

f $\triangle \times 7 = 518$

**B1** Copy and complete the ready-reckoner for these stamps.

| Buy |  |  |  |  |
|---|---|---|---|---|
| 3 | 57p | 78p | | |
| $\square$ | 76p | | 152p | 180p |
| 6 | | 156p | 228p | 270p |
| $\square$ | 171p | 234p | | |

## C1

**You need**

a partner

a 0–9 dice

these digit cards

a calculator

- Use the cards to make a 2-digit number.

- Roll the dice keeping the score secret.

- Enter the 2-digit number in the calculator.

- Multiply by the dice score.

- Show the product to your partner.

- Ask your partner to work out the number you threw.

- If your partner finds the right number, they win a point.

- The winner is the player with the most points after 10 rounds.

| **Key idea** | Sharing is better for dividing by small numbers. |
| --- | --- |
| | Grouping is better for dividing by larger numbers. |

# Multiply and divide

| **Key idea** | You can check multiplication by division. You can check division by multiplication. |
|---|---|

**A1** Dan's Diner uses all these items every 8 weeks.

  **a** How many portions of each item do they use each week?

  **b** Check your answers to **a** using multiplication.

  Show your working.

**A2** Look at the number of portions in each box.

At Kate's Café, Kate buys 8 boxes of each item.

  **a** How many portions of each item does she buy?

  **b** Check your answers to **a**.

  Show your working.

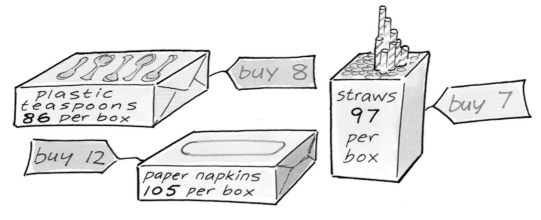

**B1** Buy these items at the Cash 'n' Carry.

> **a** Work out how many you will have of each item.

> **b** Check your answers. Show your working.

**B2** These are multiplication trios.

Find 2 integer values for each missing number.

> **a** 7, 56, △

> **b** 54, ☐, 6

> **c** 108, 9, ◯

> **d** ▱, 36, 18

> **e** 81, 3, ⬠

> **f** 121, 11, ◇

**B3** Find 1 integer value for each missing number.

> **a** △, 14, 1.4

> **b** 18, ⬡, 0.6

**C1** Find 246 × 13.

**C2** Use your answer to C1 to do these calculations.

> **a** 246 × 130 = ☐

> **b** 3198 ÷ 246 = ☐

> **c** 1.3 × 246 = ☐

> **d** 319.8 ÷ 246 = ☐

**C3** Write 3 more questions using what you found out in C1.

**C4** Choose your own starting calculation and make up 6 problems like those in C2 for a friend to solve.

| **Key idea** | You can check multiplication by division. <br> You can check division by multiplication. |

# Using factors to multiply

| Key idea | $14 \times 12 = (2 \times 7) \times 12 = 2 \times (7 \times 12) = 2 \times 84$ |
|---|---|

★1    15 x 2 = 30

Use this answer to help you work these out.

a   $15 \times 4$    b   $15 \times 8$    c   $30 \times 2$    d   $30 \times 8$

Think about the factors.

★2    Work out $15 \times 3$.

Use your answer to help you work these out.

a   $15 \times 6$    b   $15 \times 12$    c   $15 \times 9$    d   $30 \times 3$

B1    Work out $23 \times 3$.

Use your answer to help with these.

a   $23 \times 6$    b   $23 \times 9$    c   $23 \times 12$

B2    Work out $35 \times 7$.

Use your answer to help with these.

a   $35 \times 14$    b   $35 \times 21$    c   $35 \times 70$

**B3**

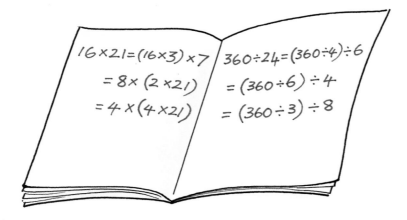

$$16 \times 21 = (16 \times 3) \times 7$$
$$= 8 \times (2 \times 21)$$
$$= 4 \times (4 \times 21)$$

$$360 \div 24 = (360 \div 4) \div 6$$
$$= (360 \div 6) \div 4$$
$$= (360 \div 3) \div 8$$

Using factors, find 3 different ways to split up each multiplication or division calculation.

a $\quad$ 12 × 18

b $\quad$ 14 × 21

c $\quad$ 18 × 16

d $\quad$ 24 × 12

e $\quad$ 25 × 15

f $\quad$ 168 ÷ 12

g $\quad$ 240 ÷ 16

h $\quad$ 384 ÷ 24

**B4** $\quad$ For each calculation in B3, choose one of your ways and work out the answer.

**C1** $\quad$ Find these differences of squares.

a $\quad$ Copy and complete the 5 rows in each column.

Column 1
$(2 \times 2) - (1 \times 1) = \square$
$(3 \times 3) - (2 \times 2) = \square$
$(4 \times 4) - (3 \times 3) = \square$
$(5 \times 5) - (4 \times 4) = \square$
$(6 \times 6) - (5 \times 5) = \square$

Column 2
$(3 \times 3) - (1 \times 1) = \square$
$(4 \times 4) - (2 \times 2) = \square$
$(5 \times 5) - (3 \times 3) = \square$
$(6 \times 6) - (4 \times 4) = \square$
$(7 \times 7) - (5 \times 5) = \square$

Column 3
$(4 \times 4) - (1 \times 1) = \square$
$(5 \times 5) - (2 \times 2) = \square$
$(6 \times 6) - (3 \times 3) = \square$
$(7 \times 7) - (4 \times 4) = \square$
$(8 \times 8) - (5 \times 5) = \square$

b $\quad$ Look for patterns in your answers.

Use the patterns to work out

• the results for row 10

• $(21 \times 21) - (20 \times 20)$ $\qquad$ $(20 \times 20) - (18 \times 18)$ $\qquad$ $(22 \times 22) - (19 \times 19)$

c $\quad$ Find a general rule for each column.

**Key idea** $\quad$ $14 \times 12 = (2 \times 7) \times 12 = 2 \times (7 \times 12) = 2 \times 84$

Multiplying decimals 1

| Key idea | Use multiplication facts you already know to multiply decimals. |
| --- | --- |

**B1** Copy these number patterns.

Complete the last 3 lines in each pattern.

**a**  $(1 \times 9) + 2 = 11$

$(12 \times 9) + 3 = 111$

$(123 \times 9) + 4 = 1111$

$(1234 \times 9) + 5 = \square$

$\square + \square = \square$

$\square + \square = \square$

**b**  $(8 \times 1) + 1 = 9$

$(8 \times 12) + 2 = 98$

$(8 \times 123) + 3 = 987$

$(8 \times 1234) + 4 = \square$

$\square + \square = \square$

$\square + \square = \square$

Do the brackets first.

**B2** Copy and complete these number patterns.

**a**  $9 \times 12 = 108$

$9 \times 23 = \square$

$9 \times 34 = \square$

⋮

$9 \times 89 = \square$

**b**  $1089 \times 1 = 1089$

$1089 \times 2 = \square$

$1089 \times 3 = \square$

⋮

$1089 \times 9 = \square$

Continue each pattern.

**B3** Use your answers in B2 to help you work these out mentally.

**a**  $12 \times 0.9 = \square$

**b**  $45 \times 0.9 = \square$

**c**  $\square \times 0.9 = 80.1$

**d**  $1089 \times 0.3 = \square$

**e**  $1089 \times \square = 544.5$

**f**  $1089 \times \square = 871.2$

**B4** Make up 4 questions like those in B3 for a friend to solve.

Work out the answers!

## MD2.2 Split numbers to multiply

| Key idea | You can multiply larger numbers by breaking them down into manageable parts. |
|---|---|

**A1** Copy and complete.

a $5^2 = \square$   b $3^2 = \square$   c $7^2 = \square$

$4^2 = 4 \times 4 = 16$

d $2^2 = \square$   e $6^2 = \square$   f $9^2 = \square$

g $8^2 = \square$   h $11^2 = \square$

**A2** Copy and complete.

a $40^2 = \square$   b $70^2 = \square$   c $50^2 = \square$

d $90^2 = \square$   e $110^2 = \square$   f $120^2 = \square$

**A3** Copy and complete the pattern.

$(1 \times 1) + 1 = (2 \times 2) - 2 = 2$

$(2 \times 2) + 2 = (3 \times 3) - 3 = 6$

$(3 \times 3) + 3 = (4 \times 4) - 4 = \square$

$\vdots \qquad \vdots$

$(9 \times 9) + 9 = (10 \times 10) - 10 = \square$

**B1** Solve the clues to find each mystery number.

a
- even
- square
- digit difference of 2

42  64  68  36

b
- odd
- square
- multiple of 3

49  63  90  81

c
- more than $96 \div 6$
- less than $288 \div 8$
- square

16  32  36  25

d
- multiple of 7
- digit sum of 6
- not a square number

42  70  56  49

**B2** Make up 2 puzzles like those in B1 for a friend to solve.

**B3** Split a number and use brackets to work out the answers.

a $37 \times 6 = \square$   b $28 \times 9 = \square$   c $46 \times 7 = \square$   d $59 \times 8 = \square$

e $43 \times 9 = \square$   f $64 \times 8 = \square$   g $42 \times 7 = \square$   h $72 \times 6 = \square$

**C1** Look at this sequence of positive integers.

1 2 3 4 5 6 ... 17 18 19 ...

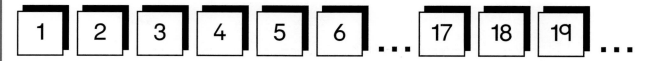

- Take any 3 consecutive numbers. 4, 5, 6
- Square the middle number. $5 \times 5 = 25$
- Multiply the first and last numbers. $4 \times 6 = 24$
- Subtract. $25 - 24 = 1$

Is the product of the first and last numbers always 1 less than the square of the middle number?

**a** Investigate for these consecutive numbers.

2, 3, 4    6, 7, 8    10, 11, 12    15, 16, 17    19, 20, 21

**b** Check with 2 sets of consecutive numbers of your choice.

**C2** This is the sequence of Fibonacci numbers.

0 1 1 2 3 5 8 13 21 34 55

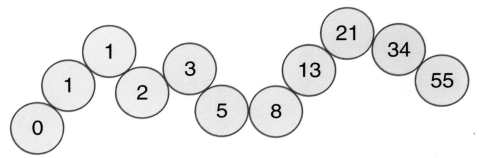

**a** Take any 3 consecutive numbers from the Fibonacci sequence.

Multiply the first and last numbers and square the middle number.

**b** What do you notice about the difference each time?

**C3** Will the rule apply to the circled Fibonacci numbers? Investigate.

**a** (2) 3 (5) 8 (13)

**b** (5) 8 (13) 21 (34)

**c** (8) 13 (21) 34 (55)

**Key idea** You can multiply larger numbers by breaking them down into manageable parts.

| Key idea | You can use a grid to help you organise parts of a multiplication. |
|---|---|

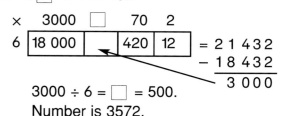

**B1**  Approximate first.

Then use the grid method to work out each calculation.

a  3142 × 4 = ☐    b  4213 × 5 = ☐    c  6123 × 6 = ☐

d  2753 × 5 = ☐    e  7235 × 7 = ☐    f  8420 × 9 = ☐

g  4802 × 9 = ☐    h  5441 × 8 = ☐    i  2814 × 7 = ☐

j  8385 × 8 = ☐    k  3588 × 6 = ☐    l  6057 × 8 = ☐

m  9219 × 7 = ☐    n  8007 × 9 = ☐    o  7250 × 5 = ☐

**C1**  Using the grid method find the missing digit.

a  4☐35 × 4 = 16 940

b  27☐8 × 6 = 16 548

c  339☐ × 7 = 23 744

d  ☐248 × 8 = 49 984

e  632☐ × 4 = 25 312

g  5☐63 × 9 = 52 767

**Example**  3☐72 = 21 432

| × | 3000 | ☐ | 70 | 2 | |
|---|---|---|---|---|---|
| 6 | 18 000 | | 420 | 12 | = 21 432 |

= 21 432
− 18 432
———————
3 000

3000 ÷ 6 = ☐ = 500.
Number is 3572.

f  95☐4 × 5 = 47 870

h  ☐472 × 8 = 67776

# Short multiplication

| Key idea | You can use columns to help you organise parts of a multiplication. |
|---|---|

**B1** You need squared paper.

First approximate your answer.

Then record your working using the column method.

**a** 2794 × 5

**b** 5348 × 6

**c** 9173 × 4

**d** 4815 × 7

**e** 6769 × 8

**f** 7826 × 3

**g** 8563 × 9

Example

4 765 × 5 ≈ 5000 × 5 = 25 000

|  |  | 4 | 7 | 6 | 5 |
|---|---|---|---|---|---|
|  | × |  |  |  | 5 |
| (4000 × 5) | 2 | 0 | 0 | 0 | 0 |
| (700 × 5) |  | 3 | 5 | 0 | 0 |
| (60 × 5) |  |  | 3 | 0 | 0 |
| (5 × 5) |  |  |  | 2 | 5 |
|  | 2 | 3 | 8 | 2 | 5 |

**B2** Approximate first, then use the short column method to work these out.

**a** 4653 × 8

**b** 8276 × 6

**c** 6435 × 9

**d** 2687 × 8

**e** 5346 × 7

**f** 7862 × 5

**Example**

```
    4 7 6 5
×         5
  2 3 8 2 5
    3 3 2
```

**C1**

**a** Copy and complete this grid.

**b** Write about any patterns you notice on the right-hand side of the grid.

| Left-hand side | | | | | | | | Right-hand side | | | | | |
|---|---|---|---|---|---|---|---|---|---|---|---|---|---|
| 7 | 6 | 9 | 2 | 3 | × | 2 | = | 1 | 5 | 3 | 8 | 4 | 6 |
| 7 | 6 | 9 | 2 | 3 | × | 7 | = | | | | | | |
| 7 | 6 | 9 | 2 | 3 | × | 5 | = | | | | | | |
| 7 | 6 | 9 | 2 | 3 | × | 11 | = | | | | | | |
| 7 | 6 | 9 | 2 | 3 | × | 6 | = | | | | | | |
| 7 | 6 | 9 | 2 | 3 | × | 8 | = | | | | | | |

# MD3.1 Division and fractions

> **Key idea** | $\frac{1}{3}$ of 24 is equivalent to $24 \div 3$ or $\frac{24}{3}$.

**★1**  **a** $\frac{1}{2}$ of $16 = \square$  **b** $16 \div 2 = \square$  **c** $\frac{16}{2} = \square$

**★2**  **a** $\frac{1}{2}$ of $24 = \square$  **b** $24 \div 2 = \square$  **c** $\frac{24}{2} = \square$

**★3**  **a** $\frac{1}{4}$ of $36 = \square$  **b** $36 \div 4 = \square$  **c** $\frac{36}{4} = \square$

**A1**  Here are 3 ways of writing the same division.

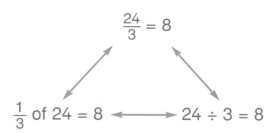

$$\frac{24}{3} = 8$$

$$\frac{1}{3} \text{ of } 24 = 8 \longleftrightarrow 24 \div 3 = 8$$

Write the 3-way relationship for each of these.

Remember to give the answers.

**a** $\frac{1}{3}$ of 18   **b** $24 \div 4$   **c** $\frac{42}{6}$

**d** $\frac{1}{8}$ of 56   **e** $36 \div 6$   **f** $\frac{64}{8}$

**g** $\frac{1}{6}$ of 60   **h** $56 \div 8$   **i** $\frac{90}{3}$

**A2**  Find $\frac{1}{3}$ of these numbers.

**a** 12   **b** 36   **c** 42

**d** 120   **e** 13   **f** 2

**A3**  Find $\frac{1}{6}$ of these numbers.

**a** 42   **b** 60   **c** 24

**d** 240   **e** 113   **f** 5

**B1**  Do CM 30.

**B2**  Copy and complete each triple.

| a | $\frac{1}{2}$ of 24 = ☐ | b | $96 \div 2 =$ ☐ | c | $\frac{56}{2} =$ ☐ |
|---|---|---|---|---|---|
|   | $\frac{1}{4}$ of 24 = ☐ |   | $96 \div 4 =$ ☐ |   | $\frac{56}{4} =$ ☐ |
|   | $\frac{1}{8}$ of 24 = ☐ |   | $96 \div 8 =$ ☐ |   | $\frac{56}{8} =$ ☐ |

**B3**  Use the pattern to work out $\frac{1}{16}$ of each number in B2.

**B4**  a  Find $\frac{1}{3}$ of each of these numbers:  **24   36   27   126   15**

  b  Find $\frac{1}{6}$ of each number in  a .

  c  Now use the pattern to work out $\frac{1}{12}$ of each number.

**B5**  **7 x 80 = 560**

  a  $\frac{1}{7}$ of 560 = ☐        b  $\frac{1}{8}$ of 560 = ☐

**B6**  **9 x 120 = 1080**

  a  $\frac{1}{9}$ of 1080 = ☐        b  $\frac{1}{12}$ of 1080 = ☐

**C1**  You need CM 31.

Make up your own hexagon division puzzles on CM 31.

Remember to work out the answers.

| **Key idea** | $\frac{1}{3}$ of 24 is equivalent to $24 \div 3$ or $\frac{24}{3}$. |
|---|---|

# MD3.2 Fraction quotients

| Key idea | Quotients can be given as mixed numbers. |
| --- | --- |

> Remember to cancel the fractions.

**A1** Find the quotients and write them as mixed numbers.

a $19 \div 7 = \square$  b $28 \div 8 = \square$  c $78 \div 9 = \square$  d $62 \div 5 = \square$

e $55 \div 7 = \square$  f $33 \div 6 = \square$  g $31 \div 8 = \square$  h $39 \div 9 = \square$

**A2** Choose one of these numbers to complete each question, then find the quotients.

## 8    7    9    6

a $46 \div \square$  b $57 \div \square$  c $62 \div \square$  d $103 \div \square$

**B1** Work out these divisions.

Write the quotients as mixed numbers.

a $97 \div 4 = \square$  b $104 \div 6 = \square$  c $267 \div 9 = \square$  d $254 \div 8 = \square$

**B2** a Use a set of digit cards numbered 0 to 9.

Shuffle the cards and take the top 4 cards.

Use the 4 numbers to make a division question like this, and find the quotient.

**2 7 3 ÷ 8**

b Repeat for 5 more different divisions.

> Think about the inverse operation.

**C1** Copy and complete these divisions.

a $\square \div 7 = 9\frac{5}{7}$  b $\square \div 9 = 3\frac{4}{9}$  c $\square \div 7 = 12\frac{4}{7}$

d $\square \div \square = 11\frac{3}{8}$  e $\square \div 4 = 12\frac{1}{2}$  f $\square \div 6 = 6\frac{1}{3}$

**C2** Each $\square$ stands for an integer. What could they be?

a $\square \div 6 = \square\frac{1}{6}$  b $\square \div 7 = \square\frac{3}{7}$  c $\square \div 8 = \square\frac{1}{4}$

Decimal quotients

| Key idea | Quotients can be given as decimals. |
|---|---|

**★1** Round these numbers to 1 decimal place.

| a | 19.37 | b | 16.44 | c | 6.72 | d | 36.15 |
|---|---|---|---|---|---|---|---|
| e | 15.89 | f | 127.26 | g | 163.45 | h | 23.07 |

**B1** Buy one of each item. The price tag shows the cost for the whole box or pack.

Work out the answers in your head.

a    b    c

d    e    f

**B2** For each calculation, write an approximate answer then work out the answer.

Show your working.

| a | 355 ÷ 5 | b | 252 ÷ 4 | c | 632 ÷ 6 | d | 914 ÷ 7 |
|---|---|---|---|---|---|---|---|
| e | 898 ÷ 8 | f | 756 ÷ 7 | g | 750 ÷ 9 | h | 472 ÷ 8 |

**B3** Use a calculator to find the quotients.

Round your answers to 1 decimal place if necessary.

| a | 369 ÷ 3 | b | 119 ÷ 2 | c | 627 ÷ 4 | d | 123 ÷ 10 | e | 493 ÷ 4 |
|---|---|---|---|---|---|---|---|---|---|
| f | 678 ÷ 5 | g | 821 ÷ 4 | h | 779 ÷ 10 | i | 631 ÷ 5 | j | 7139 ÷ 2 |

Five families win cash prizes at a school fete:

| Family | Number of people in family | Prize money |
|---|---|---|
| Walker | 5 | £52 |
| O'Doherty | 4 | £73 |
| Wang | 2 | £39 |
| McDougall | 5 | £16 |
| Patak | 4 | £49 |

Each family shares their prize money equally between the people in their family.

For example, each person in the Walker family gets £52 ÷ 5.

Find an approximate answer first.

**a** Find how much individuals receive in each family.

**b** In which family does each individual receive the most?

**c** In which family does each individual receive the least?

**Key idea** | Quotients can be given as decimals.

MD3 Fraction and decimal quotients

# Using multiples to check divisions

| Key idea | Use what you know about multiples to check that your divisions are correct. |

**A1**

# 108   155   246   376   540

Use the divisibility tests. Identify which of these numbers are:

**a** divisible by 2      **b** divisible by 5      **c** divisible by 10

**d** divisible by 4      **e** divisible by 3      **f** divisible by 6

**A2** Use short division to solve these.

**a** 108 ÷ 4      **b** 155 ÷ 5      **c** 246 ÷ 3      **d** 540 ÷ 4      **e** 376 ÷ 6

**A3** Use your answers to A1 to check your answers to A2. Explain in writing what you find.

**B1** Write a test for divisibility by 8.

**B2** **a** Copy and continue this sequence: 423, 426, 429, ... 450

**b** Identify the numbers that are divisible by 9.
Divide each of your answers to by 9.

**c** Identify the numbers that are divisible by 8.
Divide your answers to by 8.

**B3** Use short division to solve these.

**a** 703 ÷ 4      **b** 864 ÷ 6      **c** 375 ÷ 8      **d** 746 ÷ 9      **e** 921 ÷ 6

**B4** Check your answers to B3 by using tests of divisibility.

**C1** Find the missing divisors. Copy and complete.

**a** 252 ÷ ☐ ÷ ☐ = 7      **b** 174 ÷ ☐ ÷ ☐ = 29      **c** 336 ÷ ☐ ÷ ☐ = 14

**d** 432 ÷ ☐ ÷ ☐ = 72      **e** 828 ÷ ☐ ÷ ☐ = 138

**C2** Copy and complete this sentence.

The above numbers are divisible by _____ and by _____ and by _____.

# Using multiples to help you divide

| Key idea | You can use multiples to help you divide. |
|---|---|

**★1** Use grouping. Copy and complete.

**a** $80 \div 20 = \square$  **b** $120 \div 20 = \square$  **c** $150 \div 30 = \square$

**d** $450 \div 50 = \square$  **e** $240 \div 40 = \square$  **f** $600 \div 30 = \square$

**g** $350 \div 70 = \square$  **h** $630 \div 90 = \square$

**A1**

$140 \div 18$
Round 18 to 20
$140 \div 20 = 7$
Approximate answer is 7

$140 \div 18$

$\begin{array}{r} 140 \\ -126 \leftarrow \text{try 7 lots of 18} \\ \hline 14 \end{array}$

Actual answer is 7 r 14

Round the divisor to the nearest 10 to find an approximate answer.

Use the approximate answer to help with your working.

**a** $160 \div 19$  **b** $240 \div 38$  **c** $140 \div 68$  **d** $420 \div 73$

**B1** Find the approximate answer then work these out.

**a** $213 \div 29$  **b** $647 \div 52$

**c** $644 \div 44$  **d** $453 \div 87$

**e** $570 \div 15$  **f** $525 \div 21$

**g** $627 \div 19$  **h** $832 \div 32$

Remember to keep the digits in the correct columns

$954 \div 18 \approx 1000 \div 20 = 50$

$\begin{array}{r} 954 \\ -360 \ (20 \times 18) \\ \hline 594 \\ -360 \ (20 \times 18) \\ \hline 234 \\ -180 \ (10 \times 18) \\ \hline 54 \\ -54 \ (3 \times 18) \\ \hline 0 \end{array}$

Answer : 53

**B2** Sally's scooter travels 27 km on 1 litre of petrol.

She travels 351 km each month going to work and back.

How many litres does she use each month for these journeys?

Approximate first.

**B3** 884 people watched the school concert.

The chairs were arranged in rows of 34.

All the seats were taken, so how many rows of chairs were there?

**C1** Solve these and explain how the first answer helped you complete the second calculation.

Choose a method of recording which you find easiest.

| | 1st calculation | 2nd calculation |
|---|---|---|
| a | 760 ÷ 10 | 760 ÷ 5 |
| b | 168 ÷ 12 | 168 ÷ 24 |
| c | 774 ÷ 18 | 774 ÷ 36 |
| d | 825 ÷ 25 | 825 ÷ 75 |

**C2** Does the first answer help you with the second in this case?

674 ÷ 32          674 ÷ 64

**Key idea** You can use multiples to help you divide.

# Introducing long division

| Key idea | Use your multiplication facts to help you with long division. |
| --- | --- |

**★1** Use long division to do these.

**a** 614 ÷ 20     **b** 832 ÷ 30     **c** 746 ÷ 40

**A1** Copy and complete.

**a**
```
        □□  r □
13 ) 1 5 8
   − 1 3 0    10 × 13
     2 8
   − □□     □ × 13
     □
```

**b**
```
        □□  r □
25 ) 5 4 7
   − □□□    20 × 25
     □□
   − □□     □ × 25
     □□
```

**A2** Use long division to find out how many seats there are in each row.

**a** There are 864 people on a full ship.

There are 36 rows of seats.

**b** There are 918 people in a cinema.

There are 27 rows of seats.

You need a calculator.

**B1** Use long division to do these.

**a** 558 ÷ 31     **b** 418 ÷ 19     **c** 714 ÷ 42     **d** 302 ÷ 16

**B2** Use a calculator to check your answer to B1 **a**, using the inverse operation. Record how you do this.

**B3** Use long division to do these.

**a** 773 ÷ 34     **b** 428 ÷ 36     **c** 943 ÷ 45     **d** 846 ÷ 73

**B4** Use multiplication to check your answer to B3 **a**.

Record how you do this.

Mr George has owned his car for 2 years.

In that time he has used £984 worth of petrol.

If he uses the same amount each month, how much has he used each month?

You need a calculator.

**C1**　Find the missing numbers.

**a**　□ ÷ 35 = 36 $\frac{2}{35}$

**b**　842 ÷ □ = 38 r □

**C2**　Find 3 different pairs of numbers to make this correct.

□ □ 6 □ ÷ □ □ = 2 4

Use divisibility
tests to help you.

**Key idea**　Use your multiplication facts to help you with long division.

Using known facts

| Key idea | Use multiplication facts you know to help you work out new facts. |

**A1** Make number sentences by matching pairs of number statements.

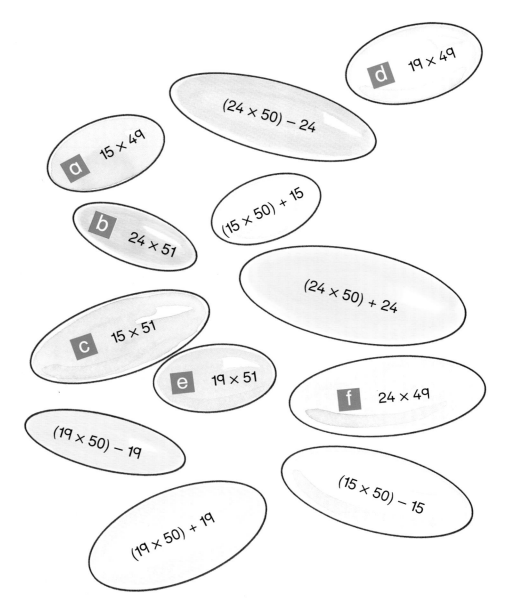

d  19 × 49

(24 × 50) − 24

a  15 × 49

(15 × 50) + 15

b  24 × 51

(24 × 50) + 24

c  15 × 51

e  19 × 51

f  24 × 49

(19 × 50) − 19

(15 × 50) − 15

(19 × 50) + 19

**A2** Find the answers to the multiplications in A1.

**B1** Marvin is restocking his shop.

What is the total cost of each item?

| Item | Quantity | Price per item | Total in £ |
|---|---|---|---|
| | 99 | 25p | a |
| | 101 | 79p | b |
| | 99 | 44p | c |
| | 101 | 56p | d |
| | 99 | 63p | e |
| | 101 | 92p | f |
| | 99 | £1.50 | g |

**C1** Copy and complete.

**a** 367 × 99 = ☐     **b** 384 × 101 = ☐     **c** 761 × 51 = ☐

**d** 438 × 49 = ☐     **e** 639 × 51 = ☐     **f** 932 × 49 = ☐

**Key idea** | Use multiplication facts you know to help you work out new facts.

# Checking results

| **Key idea** | Do the calculation in a different way to check your answer. |

**A1** Marvin does some calculations for his tricks.

Copy and complete his working.

 **a**  18 × 47

$18 \times 47 = (18 \times 50) - 54$
$= \boxed{\phantom{0}} - 54$
$= \boxed{\phantom{0}}$

**b** 26 × 52

$26 \times 52 = (26 \times 50) + \boxed{\phantom{0}}$
$= \boxed{\phantom{0}} + \boxed{\phantom{0}}$
$= \boxed{\phantom{0}}$

**c** 16 × 45

$16 \times 45 = (16 \times 50) - \boxed{\phantom{0}}$
$= \boxed{\phantom{0}} - \boxed{\phantom{0}}$
$= \boxed{\phantom{0}}$

**d**  24 × 53

$24 \times 53 = \underline{\hspace{3cm}}$
$= \underline{\hspace{3cm}}$
$= \boxed{\phantom{0}}$

**A2** Use an equivalent calculation to check your answers to A1.

**B1** For each question, choose the method that you think is best.

Approximate first.

**a** $73 \times 29 = \square$    **b** $65 \times 42 = \square$    **c** $81 \times 38 = \square$

**d** $184 \times 98 = \square$    **e** $374 \times 15 = \square$    **f** $425 \times 22 = \square$

**g** $372 \times 31 = \square$    **h** $576 \times 51 = \square$    **i** $764 \times 72 = \square$

**B2** Check your answers to B1 using an equivalent calculation.

Show what you do.

**C1** For each question, choose the method that you think is best.

Approximate first.

**a** $1914 \times 6$

**b** $1246 \times 8$

**c** $5175 \times 23$

**d** $3142 \times 14$

**e** $263 \times \square 5 = 9205$

**f** $1 \square 4 \times 18 = 2952$

**C2** Check your answers to C1 using equivalent calculations.

| Key idea | Do the calculation in a different way to check your answer. |
| --- | --- |

# MD5.3 Multiplying decimals 2

> **Key idea** Use columns to help you organise parts of a multiplication.

**A1** Find the answers, using a written column method.

Approximate first.

**a** 343 × 6

**b** 517 × 4

**c** 4294 × 8

**d** 6497 × 5

**e** 8791 × 9

**B1**

**a** 2.47 × 5

**b** 4.28 × 6

**c** 7.75 × 5

**d** 5.15 × 7

**e** 6.07 × 9

**f** 7.25 × 9

**g** 3.68 × 4

**h** 8.32 × 8

**C1** You need digit cards.

**a** Pick 4 digit cards. Use them to make 6 multiplications like those in B1.

**b** What is the largest product you can make?

**c** What is the smallest product you can make?

# MD6.1 Using a calculator to divide

| **Key idea** | You can check a division by estimating the answer before calculating exactly. |
|---|---|

★1    Round these numbers to the nearest whole number.

a   12.6         b   142.5         c   34.46

d   91.3         e   15.62         f   83.01

You need a calculator.

**A1**   Estimate these quotients and then find the answers using a calculator.

a   180 ÷ 4         b   248 ÷ 6         c   511 ÷ 5

d   98 ÷ 3         e   329 ÷ 3         f   76 ÷ 5

**A2**   Where the answers to A1 are not integers, round them to the nearest whole number.

**A3**   Copy and complete these divisions. Round each answer to 1 decimal place.

a   753 ÷ 6 = ☐      b   456 ÷ 25 = ☐      c   961 ÷ 33 = ☐

**B1**

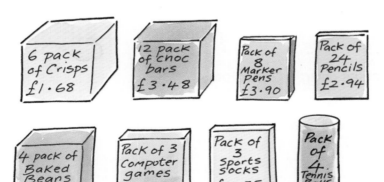

6 pack of Crisps £1·68    12 pack of choc bars £3·48    Pack of 8 Marker Pens £3·90    Pack of 24 Pencils £2·94

4 pack of Baked Beans £1·25    Pack of 3 Computer games £27·99    Pack of 3 Sports Socks £11·75    Pack of 4 Tennis Balls £9·99

a   Estimate the cost of one of each item.

b   Use a calculator to find the exact cost.

c   Is each exact cost a sensible price, or do you need to round it?

**B2**   Each of the multi-packs has an extra item free.

What is the cost of each item in the pack now?

Get one free

You need a calculator.

**C1** 6W are planning a disco. Here are the costs.

Hire of hall £155.00          DJ and disco £108.00          Lighting £72.00

They don't want to make much profit, but they do need to make sure that they don't lose money.

The price of tickets will depend on how many people they expect to come.

Make some estimates of what they should charge if they expect these numbers.

**a** 320 people          **b** 60 people          **c** 120 people

**C2** Check your estimates using a calculator.

**C3** Estimate how many people would need to come if each ticket cost

**a** £3          **b** £5          **c** £6          **d** £15

**C4** Check your estimates using a calculator.

**C5** Say which solution you think is best and why you think this.

| Key idea | You can check a division by estimating the answer before calculating exactly. |

# MD6.2 Short division and decimals

| Key idea | You can use multiples of numbers to divide. |
|---|---|

You need a calculator.

★1 Estimate the answers to these divisions.

**a** 2.4 ÷ 4     **b** 3.5 ÷ 5     **c** 12.6 ÷ 2     **d** 16.2 ÷ 3

★2 Use your calculator to find the quotients in ★1.

Write down the multiplication tables you need to answer these questions.

You need a calculator.

A1 **a** It was Jo's birthday. Hamish, Dawn, Becky, Louisa and Jo went to Paul's Pizza Parlour for lunch.

The bill for the meal came to £41.20.

If they split the bill equally, how much would each of them have to pay?

**b** Hamish, Dawn, Becky and Louisa decided to pay for Jo's meal.
They shared the cost equally between the 4 of them.

How much did they each have to pay now?

A2 Work out these quotients.

**a** 9.44 ÷ 4     **b** 1.44 ÷ 4     **c** 33.66 ÷ 7     **d** 29.36 ÷ 8

A3 Write number stories in real life settings that use the divisions in A2.

**Special offer**

You need a calculator.

**B1** CDs cost £12.95 each or £37.50 if you buy 3 at the same time.

> **a** If you do buy 3 at £37.50, how much will you be paying for each CD?

> **b** How much will you save compared with buying them one at a time?

**B2** Videos are on special offer: £46.49 for 5.

They are usually £9.75 each.

> **a** How much will you save by buying 5 at the same time?

> **b** What will be the cost of each video?

**B3** Bean toys are also on special offer. They are either £4.99 each or 6 for £27.90.

> **a** How much will you save if you buy 6?

> **b** You want to buy 11. What is the cheapest way to buy them?

You need a calculator.

**C1** The local sports shop has an end of season sale and is reducing all marked prices by 25%!

How much will each of these items cost in the sale?

| Dartboard £24.92 | Football £18.68 | Rugby ball £17.35 | Basketball net £47.65 | Badmington racket £12.99 |

**C2** What would the sale prices have been for the items if the sale had taken $\frac{1}{3}$ off marked prices?

| **Key idea** | You can use multiples of numbers to divide. |

# Choosing appropriate methods to divide

| Key idea | Choose the most appropriate way to do a calculation. |
|---|---|

**Which method is best for you?**

Work with a partner.

For each question below, decide which method of division you think is most suitable.

Solve the problem showing any working you do.

1   Sam has 38p. How many 4p stickers can he buy?

2   Milk bottles are packed in crates of 20. How many crates are needed for 138 bottles?

3   For the school play 630 tickets have been sold.

   If there are 35 seats in a row, how many rows are needed?

4   If the area of a rectangle is 54 m² and the length is 9 m, what is the width?

5   Which is the best buy: 328 marbles for 82p or 256 marbles for 74p?

6   The cost of a family holiday is £850.
   The family manages to save £34 per week.

   How long will it take them to save for the holiday?

**7** Eggs are packed in boxes of 12. How many boxes will 400 eggs fill?

**8** If $1\frac{1}{2}$ litres of milk cost £1.20, what does 1 litre cost?

**9** How many 25 cm pieces of string can be cut from 8 metres of string?

**10** Tommy can't wait for his birthday and asks his dad how long it is until it is here. His dad tells him it is 912 hours!

What is this in weeks and days?

**11** If 30 chocolate bars cost £12.60, how much does each one cost?

**12** A car is travelling at 90 km per hour.

How far will it travel in 10 minutes?

**13** In a school of 1134 children, one sixth ( $\frac{1}{6}$ ) don't like PE. How many children is this?

**14** There are 22 slices of bread in a loaf.

How many loaves are needed for 32 children to have 2 sandwiches each? (A sandwich uses 2 slices of bread.)

**15** A school outing to the museum cists £94.50 altogether.

If 18 children go on the trip what is the cost for each child?

| Key idea | Choose the most appropriate way to do a calculation. |
| --- | --- |

# Solving problems using division

| Key idea | When using division to solve problems, make sensible decisions about rounding up or down. |
|---|---|

Work with a partner.

You may need to use the information from one question to help with another, so hunt around for what you need and don't forget what you have already found out as you move on!

**1** There are 348 children at Bramley Hall School.
As luck would have it, there are 29 children in every class.

How many classes are there?

**2** The children sit at tables in groups of 4.

How many tables are needed in each class?

> You may need information from an earlier question to help you.

**3** One third of the children at Bramley Hall are in the infants.
Half the children in the juniors at Bramley Hall are boys.

How many girls are there in the juniors?

**4** Last term the school had a non-uniform day. Each class raised £43.50.

How much did each child pay?

**5** The school used the money raised from the non-uniform day in the following ways:
- It donated $\frac{1}{6}$ of the money to a local charity.
- It spent $\frac{1}{2}$ of the money on improving the environmental area.
- $\frac{1}{3}$ was put towards buying new books for the school library.

**a** How much money was raised altogether?

**b** How much was donated to the local charity?

**c** How much was given to the environmental area?

**d** How many books costing £5.99 were bought?

**e** How much money was left over?

**6** 33 children and 5 adults from Bramley Hall School rugby club are going to the match. They will travel in the school minibus, which seats 16 people.

How many trips will the minibus have to make to get everyone to the match?

**7** The Lightning Lizards' ground can hold 1248 people when it is full. It has 4 stands.

How many spectators can each stand hold?

**8** Only 840 supporters arrive to watch this local derby.

What is the average number of people in each stand?

> You may need information from an earlier question to help you.

**9** One fifth of the fans support the Racing Rhinos.

How many support the Lightning Lizards?

**10** If there are 31 seats in a row, how many whole rows are there in each of the stands?

**11** It costs Bramley Hall £53.75 for their group to watch the match. The adults' tickets cost £2.50 each.

How much does a child's ticket cost?

**12** The group from the school rugby club has £30.00 to spend on refreshments. Everyone has a cola costing 45p. They decide to spend the rest of their money on chocolate bars, which cost 36p each.

How many chocolate bars can they buy?

**13** This season the Lightning Lizards have decided to pledge some money to charity. They ask every spectator to give 5p as they come through the gates. The club itself donates 8p for every 5p given by a spectator. Last week they raised £87.10 with this scheme.

How many supporters took part?

**14** Ticket prices for the concert were £9.50 standing, £15 seated.
Tickets were sold for all 2600 seats.

How much money was taken from the sale of the 'seated' tickets?

**15** The total ticket sales were £46 068.

How many 'standing' tickets were sold?

**16** A transport survey of the people who bought tickets for the standing area found that
• 50% came by train
• one third came by coach
• the remainder came by car.

How many people used each type of transport?

**17** Parking was a problem. The organisers estimated that there would be 1100 cars arriving.
The field they used for parking accommodates 35 cars in a row.

How many rows were needed?

**18** Programme sales raised £9485.

How many were sold if programmes cost £7?

**19** The band decided that 5% of the money taken from programme sales would be donated to a local charity.

How much was donated?

**20** One quarter of all the fans at the concert bought a CD at the souvenir stand. One eighth bought a T-shirt.

**a** How many CDs were sold?

**b** How many T-shirts were sold?

| **Key idea** | When using division to solve problems, make sensible decisions about rounding up or down. |
|---|---|

# Using an approximate answer

| Key idea | Remember to check the size of your exact answer against your approximate answer. |
| --- | --- |

**★1**

| | | | |
| --- | --- | --- | --- |
| 2.25 × 5 | 5.78 × 8 | 4.98 × 7 | |
| 3.11 × 9 | | 8.21 × 4 | |
| | 7.02 × 3 | | |

| | | |
| --- | --- | --- |
| 27.99 | 11.25 | 21.06 |
| 46.24 | | 32.84 |
| | 34.86 | |

Match each multiplication to its answer like this:

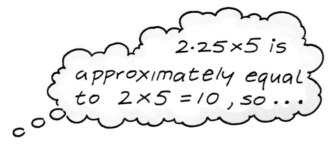

2.25 × 5 is approximately equal to 2×5 =10, so...

2.25 × 5 = 11.25

**A1** Write approximate answers to these.

a 6.7 × 3    b 4.12 × 3    c 2.95 × 5    d 3.44 × 7

**A2** ◯ stands for a whole number in each number sentence.

Round both of the other numbers in each sentence either up or down to help you find the missing numbers.

a 5.54 × ◯ = 43.32

b 2.88 × ◯ = 17.28

Use other clues to check that you are probably correct.

c ◯ × 4.05 = 28.35

**A3** Find an approximate answer first, then work out the exact answer.

a 2.4 × 3    b 2.41 × 3    c 3.81 × 4

d 2.85 × 2    e 4.17 × 6    f 3.64 × 3

**B1** Find an approximate answer first, then work out the exact answer.

**a** 5.14 × 7    **b** 2.71 × 8    **c** 4.55 × 6

**d** 3.42 × 9    **e** 1.03 × 9    **f** 2.68 × 5

Compare your answers with your approximations.

They should be close!

**B2**

£4.89          £7.48          £3.62          £8.76

How much are these altogether?

**a** 6 sets of pastels    **b** 4 books    **c** 5 CDs    **d** 3 craft sets

**C1** Sam got most of her homework wrong.

• She did not know roughly how big her answers should be.

• She did not line up all the digits correctly.

```
ⓐ   2.76        ⓑ   3.98        ⓒ   8.57
   ×    5           ×    4           ×    9
   10.00           12.00          72.00
    3.50           36.00           4.50
     .30            3.20           0.63
   13.80           51.20          77.13

ⓓ   6.04        ⓔ   2.77        ⓕ   4.85
   ×    6           ×    8           ×    7
   36.00           16.00          28.00
    2.40           56.0            5.60
   38.40            .56             .35
                  216.56         289.10
```

Use any clues to tell you which are wrong at a glance.

Write down the letters of the incorrect answers.

**C2** Do Sam's corrections for her.

Choose how to set them out.

You may use Sam's way if you like it.

| **Key idea** | Remember to check the size of your exact answer against your approximate answer. |
| --- | --- |

| **Key idea** | You can adapt a standard column method for TU × TU to multiply larger numbers. |
|---|---|

★1

These are the maximum numbers of computers a warehouse can sell each month.

How many computers are needed in

a   Cambridge over 10 months?

b   Hull over 4 months?

c   Cambridge over 6 months?

d   Brighton over 12 months?

e   Hull over 15 months?

Choose the easiest way for you to multiply.

★2   If you did not use a column method for any parts of ★1, try it for them now.

**Examples**

a
```
  Th H  T  U
      3  2  1
×         1  0
   3  2  1  0
```

d
```
  Th H  T  U
         9  4
×        1  2
      1  8  8   (94 × 2)
+  ☐ ☐    0   (94 × 10)
   ☐ ☐ ☐ ☐
```

A1   • Write an approximate answer for parts a to d .

• Use columns to work them out: Th H T U

a
```
   3 1 2
×      8
```

b
```
    2 6
×  4 3
```

c
```
   2 3 4
×    2 1
```

d
```
   4 2 0
×    6 2
```

**A2** Do A1 again but use a grid method to check your answers.

**A3** Write a word problem for each calculation in A1.

IP 15 might help.

**B1** Use columns to do these calculations.

**a** 316 × 23      **b** 504 × 32      **c** 296 × 45      **d** 609 × 28

**B2** There are 423 paperclips in a full box.

**a** How many in 36 boxes?

**b** Creativecomputers.com needs to order at least 10 000 paperclips.

If they order 25 boxes will they have enough?

**c** There are 56 sheets in a memo pad.

How many in 635 pads?

**d** 52 cars can park in each row of the company car park. There are 115 rows.

How many cars can park before it is full?

**C1** Files can be packed in boxes of 24, 48, 50 or 100.

Creativecomputers.com has ordered 12 000.

**a** Find 4 ways to pack the order each using 1 size of box, with each box full and no files left out.

**b** Find ways using more than 1 size of box.

Can you find ways that use 2, 3, and 4 sizes of box?

| **Key idea** | You can adapt a standard column method for TU × TU to multiply larger numbers. |

# More long multiplication

| Key idea | Record neatly in columns to reduce mistakes in long multiplication. |
|---|---|

**★1**

a
```
  2 6 1
×    4 0
```

b
```
  3 7 6
×    5 0
```

c
```
  7 4 2
×    6 0
```

d
```
  9 5 4
×    7 0
```

**A1**

a
```
  2 6 1
×    4 1
```

b
```
  3 7 6
×    5 1
```

c
```
  7 4 2
×    6 3
```

d
```
  9 5 4
×    7 2
```

**B1** Do CM 37.

**B2** Storage boxes are stacked in piles of 44.

How many boxes are in 199 piles?

**B3**

Find out if these customers have bought enough packs.
If not, how many more do they need?

a Jarvis & Sons need 17 000 white envelopes.

They buy 26 packs.

b A library needs to store 5440 CDs and buys 156 CD boxes.

c A school needs 2546 ink cartridges. It buys 112 packs.

d Mr Patel needs 1000 sheets of paper and buys 58 pads.

**C1** Make up problems for your partner that need several calculations to solve them. Include long multiplication.

Find the answer before you swap.

# Finding more fractions

| Key idea | You can find more fractions by halving those you already know. |
|---|---|

**A1** Copy and complete.

**a** $\frac{1}{5}$ of 250 = ☐    What is $\frac{1}{10}$ of 250?

**b** $\frac{1}{3}$ of 360 = ☐    What is $\frac{1}{6}$ of 360?    What is $\frac{1}{12}$ of 360?

**c** $\frac{1}{5}$ of 82 = ☐    What is $\frac{1}{20}$ of 820?

**A2** This is a fraction machine.

It always bites off more than it can chew!

Each time it eats anything, it spits out **half** of it.

Work out how much it will spit out each time if it eats these amounts.

**a** $\frac{1}{2}$ of 40    **b** $\frac{1}{3}$ of 60    **c** $\frac{1}{6}$ of 120    **d** $\frac{1}{5}$ of 100    **e** $\frac{1}{10}$ of 80

**B1** What is    **a** $\frac{1}{12}$ of £150?    **b** $\frac{1}{6}$ of 2.1?    **c** $\frac{1}{20}$ of £450?    **d** $\frac{1}{40}$ of 3000?

**B2** 12 people shared a prize of £243. How much did they each get?

**B3** Sarah was on a 9.8 km walk.

**a** After 10 minutes she had covered $\frac{1}{20}$ of the distance. How far had she walked?

**b** How far had she walked when she had covered $\frac{11}{20}$ of the distance?

**B4** Sam wanted to cut a 3.7 m plank into equal pieces.

**a** If she made 5 equal pieces, what is the length of each piece?

**b** How many pieces would she have if each piece was 185 mm long?

**C1** **a** What fractions of amounts other than sixths, twelfths and twentieths can you find by halving fractions that you know?

**b** Make up 3 fraction machines like that in A2 with 5 questions for each machine.

# MD8.3 Using multiples of 10 and 100

| Key idea | You can use place value to multiply or divide by 10 and 100. |
|---|---|

**A1** Multiply each number by 10 and then by 100. Try to do this in your head.

| a | 125 | b | 1567 | c | 8.3 | d | 0.95 | e | 624 |
|---|---|---|---|---|---|---|---|---|---|

**A2** Divide each number by 10 and then by 100. Remember to calculate mentally!

| a | 464 | b | 2673 | c | 6.8 | d | 9 | e | 74 |
|---|---|---|---|---|---|---|---|---|---|

**A3** Copy and complete.

**a** 34.3 ÷ 10 = ☐   **b** 70.2 × 100 = ☐   **c** 102.01 × 100 = ☐   **d** 7.04 × 10 = ☐

**B1** Copy and complete these multiplication and division number sentences.

**Example**
67.8 ÷ 10 = 6.78

**a** 7.24 ☐ ☐ = 0.724    **b** 75.8 ☐ ☐ = 7580

**c** 632 ☐ ☐ = 6.32    **d** 5.98 ☐ ☐ = 598

**e** 6.7 ☐ ☐ = 0.067

**B2** As the numbers go through this function machine, they are multiplied and divided as shown.

Work out what comes out when these numbers are put in .

| a | 6.4 | b | 10.3 | c | 234 | d | 5.85 | e | 40.07 |
|---|---|---|---|---|---|---|---|---|---|

**B3**   232 people are coming to watch the school play.

The chairs in the hall fit in rows of 10.

How many rows of chairs are needed?

**B4**   Make up a division question where it is sensible to round down for the answer.

**C1**   Calculate what comes out of the function machine when these numbers are put in.

| a | 65 | b | 152 | c | 8.6 | d | 10.25 | e | 20.02 |

**C2**   Make up a function machine of your own.

| Key idea | You can use place value to multiply or divide by 10 and 100. |

# SP1.1 Solving mathematical puzzles

| Key idea | Think about how numbers behave in calculations when you solve puzzles with missing digits. |
|---|---|

You need a calculator.

**★1** Find the missing digits.

a $\square 6 \times \triangle = 230$     b $\square 4 \times \triangle = 162$     c $\square \times \triangle 9 = 261$

**★2** What if ... the answers in ★1 were 10 times bigger?

Write new number sentences like this: $\square 6 \times \triangle 0 = 2300$

**A1** **Thirty-somethings**

For each of these numbers find a product like this:

$3\square \times \square\square$

1976    2211    2856

2592

Use a calculator.

**A2** Find another solution for $3\square \times \square\square = 2592$

**A3** What if ... you changed some of the 'thirty-somethings' to 'forty-somethings'?

Find the new products.

a $4\square \times \square\square = 2856$     b $4\square \times \square\square = 2592$

You need a calculator.

**B1** Find the missing digits.

a $\square 3\square \times \square\square = 9612$     b $\square 4\square \times \square\square = 53\,424$

**B2**  **a**  $\triangle\,\triangle \times \triangle = 171$

Find the missing digits.

There's more than 1 solution.
Find as many as you can.

**b**  Do you think you have found all the solutions in **a** ?

Explain why.

**c**  What if ... $\diamond\,\diamond\,\diamond \times \diamond\,\diamond = 17\ 100$ ?

Find all the solutions.

**C1**  **a**  Find 2 numbers with a product of 980.

**b**  Now find as many different pairs as you can.

Use patterns and
be systematic.

**C2**  Repeat C1 but find number trios with the same product.

| Key idea | Think about how numbers behave in calculations when you solve puzzles with missing digits. |
|---|---|

# Choosing appropriate number operations

| Key idea | Think about the effect of a number operation when you interpret word problems. |
|---|---|

**A1** Choose the operation that makes each number sentence correct.

$$+ \quad \div \quad \times \quad -$$

**a** 26 ☐ 92 = 2392

**b** 411 ☐ 86 = 325

**c** 405 ☐ 369 = 774

**d** 4424 ☐ 56 = 79

**A2** Cornflakes come in 3 different sized packets:

**a** Syrfeeta buys 1 packet of each size.
How much does she spend altogether?

*Write a number sentence for each answer.*

**b** How many grams of cornflakes does she have altogether?

**c** She eats 30 g of cornflakes each morning. How much does she eat in a week?

**d** If she eats from the largest box, what weight of cornflakes is left at the end of the week?

**e** Karl opens the 500 g box and eats 40 g a day.
Will there be enough in the box to last him a fortnight?

**f** Make up a cornflakes question of your own for your partner to solve.

**B1** Solve these problems.

- Find the key information.
- Decide which operation to use.
- Use number sentences to record your working.

**a** 95 children are going on summer camp.
They are each given a T-shirt.
If T-shirts come in packs of 6, how many packs will be needed?

**b** The children travelled the 175 km to camp by minibus.
They travelled at 50 km per hour and had a lunch stop of 45 minutes in the middle of the journey.
How long did the journey take?

**c** The children are nine, ten or eleven years old.
5 of them are nine, $\frac{3}{10}$ of the remainder are ten.
How many eleven year olds are there?

**d** The minibuses that took the children to camp each held 15 passengers.
At least one adult had to travel in each bus.
How many minibuses were needed altogether?

**B2** The answer to a number problem is '60 chose horse riding'.
What do you think the problem might have been?

**C1** Use the prime numbers 2, 3, 5 and 7 and any operations to complete the following number statements.

**Example** 2 + 3 + 5 + 7 = 17

**a** □ ☆ □ ☆ □ ☆ □ = 7     **b** □ ☆ □ ☆ □ ☆ □ = 18

**c** □ ☆ □ ☆ □ ☆ □ = 30     **d** □ ☆ □ ☆ □ ☆ □ = 16

**e** □ ☆ □ ☆ □ ☆ □ = 210

**C2** Make up some of your own using 4 different prime numbers.

**Key idea** | Think about the effect of a number operation when you interpret word problems.

# Choosing the best way to calculate

| Key idea | Decide the best way for you to calculate when you solve a problem. |
|---|---|

Work with a partner.

Jacob and Zak are shopping for their friends.

They need some help to work out how much they are spending.

They need 29 rubbers at 49p each.

15 notebooks at £1.50 each

They want 30 pencils, but they came in boxes of 12 at 99p a box.

Dictionaries are £9.95 or £5.50. Which ones can they afford if they want 6 and have £50 to spend?

21 rulers needed – 75p or £1.05 each. How much do they save if they buy the cheaper ones?

14 rolls of Sellotape – 35p a roll, or 40p a roll with a 3rd one free when they buy 2. Which do they choose?

25 pencil sharpeners at 62p each

They have £18.20 left. How many staplers can they buy at £5.99 each?

# Choosing the best way to multiply and divide

| Key idea | The best way to multiply or divide numbers depends on what the numbers are. |
|---|---|

Do the calculations mentally using jottings to help you.

Make sure someone else can understand what you have written.

**A1**   Use factors for these.

> **Example**   $13 \times 6 = 13 \times (3 \times 2)$
> $\qquad\qquad\quad = (13 \times 3) \times 2$

a   $13 \times 6$          b   $23 \times 12$          c   $25 \times 9$          d   $31 \times 18$

> **Example**   $96 \div 6 = 96 \div 3 \div 2$

e   $96 \div 6$          f   $180 \div 12$          g   $243 \div 9$          h   $306 \div 18$

> Multiplying by the largest factor first is often best but you may find it easier to divide by the smallest one first.

**A2**   Split the smaller number into tens and units to multiply these.

> **Example**
> $21 \times 12 = (21 \times 10) + (21 \times 2)$

a   $21 \times 12$          b   $23 \times 15$          c   $24 \times 14$          d   $36 \times 13$

**A3**

Use multiples of the divisor to divide these.

**Example**

$144 \div 12$

$$
\begin{array}{r}
1\ 4\ 4 \\
-\ \ 1\ 2\ 0 \quad 12 \times 10 \\
\hline
2\ 4 \\
-\ \ \ 2\ 4 \quad 12 \times 2 \\
\hline
0
\end{array}
$$

a  $144 \div 12$  b  $112 \div 14$  c  $180 \div 15$  d  $288 \div 18$

**B1**

Calculate these by splitting the smaller number or by using factors.

a  $34 \times 18$  b  $41 \times 18$  c  $27 \times 15$  d  $42 \times 24$

**B2**

Did you use the same method for all parts of B1?

Explain why you did or why you did not.

**B3**

Make up a multiplication calculation of your own and do it 2 ways:

a  split one number  b  use factors

c  Write a sentence to explain which method you think is easier.

**B4**

Choose any 2 of the multiplications that you have done so far.

Work them out using the standard column method.

Say which method you prefer for each and why.

**B5**

Calculate these by using multiples of the divisor or by using factors.

a  $378 \div 18$  b  $416 \div 16$  c  $315 \div 35$  d  $648 \div 24$

**B6**

Did you use the same method for all parts of B5?

Explain why you did or why you did not.

**C1**  Write down what you think the original multiplications were.

**a**

I multiplied it by 10, which was 240.
I halved 240 and added the two answers together.

**b**

I multiplied it by 10, which was 320.
I multiplied it by 3 and then added the two answers together.

**c**

I multiplied it by 20, which was 860.
I multiplied it by 6 and then added the two answers together.

**C2**  Work out the missing multipliers.

**a**  $22 \times ? \times ? = 198$

**b**  $23 \times ? \times ? = 276$

**c**  $24 \times ? \times ? = 288$

Remember that division is the inverse of multiplication.

**d**  $24 \times ? \times ? = 360$

**e**  Make up some of your own for your partner to solve.

| Key idea | The best way to multiply or divide numbers depends on what the numbers are. |

# SP2.2  Solving word problems

| Key idea | Read a word problem carefully to decide how many steps are needed to solve it and which number operations to use. |
| --- | --- |

★1  Each litre of minestrone soup uses 50 g of pasta.

How much pasta is needed for 12 litres of soup?

★2  There are 30 g of beans in each litre of soup.

What weight of beans is there in 15 litres?

★3  Make up your own simple cooking problems and ask your partner to solve them.

A1  Minestrone soup needs equal quantities of beans, peas and carrots.

Each litre of soup contains 30 g of carrots.

What weight of peas is there in 15 litres of soup?

A2  What is the total weight of carrots and peas in 10 litres of soup?

A3  How many litres of soup can you make with 120 g of beans?

A4  Each litre of soup serves 6 people.

148 people eat soup.

How many litres are needed?

A5  A bowl of soup costs £3.29.

What is the cost of 6 servings altogether?

Pauline delivers pizzas.
She can carry up to 6 family-sized, up to 8 large and up to 10 regular pizzas.

**B1**  Regular pizzas cost £5.55.

How many can you buy with £50?

**B2**  Today Pauline could have carried 4 more family-sized pizzas on her bike.
$\frac{1}{2}$ of the orders were for regular pizzas, $\frac{1}{10}$ were for family-sized and the rest were for large pizzas.

How many of each size did she have to deliver?

**B3**  A pizza order takes 30 minutes to make and 2 minutes to pack.

Pauline can reach her destination in 7 minutes if the traffic lights are green and 9 minutes if they are not.

When would she arrive with the pizzas if the order was placed at:

a  8:23 p.m. (the lights were red)        b  9:15 p.m. (the lights were green)

**B4**  Jodie's order totals £18.05 but she does not have the exact money.

She has a £20 note and a few coins: one 10p, four 1p and one 2p.

Pauline only has pound coins and 50p pieces.

What does Jodie give Pauline to get the right change?

Explain all your answers using number or word sentences.

**C1**   On Monday, Paul made £244 from his party menus.

20 people ate them.

How many had menu 1 and how many had menu 2?

**C2**   On Tuesday, Paul made £366 from party menus.

He thought that 26 people had chosen party menus, but Pauline said that it must be 27.

Who was right?

**C3**   On Wednesday, 25 people had party menus.

If both menus were chosen, how much might Paul have made?

What is the most money he could have made?

**C4**   Make up your own multi-step problems for Thursday, Friday and Saturday (and solve them!)

| Key idea | Read a word problem carefully to decide how many steps are needed to solve it and which number operations to use. |
| --- | --- |

# Using written methods for money problems

| Key idea | It is often efficient to use standard written methods for solving money problems with several stages. |

You need to refer to IP 16 to find out prices at Paul's Pizza Parlour.

**B1**  Sintharan eats a regular cheese dream pizza and coleslaw.

Michael chooses a large minestrone soup and garlic bread.

> coleslaw 49p
> garlic bread £1.12

**a**  Who pays more?   **b**  How much more?

**B2**  4 friends eat at Paul's.

They choose a large Hawaiian pizza, a large spaghetti bolognese and a regular barbecue pizza.

They decide to split the bill equally between the 4 of them.

How much does each pay?

**B3**  Emma and Tasha have 2 large spaghetti bolognese and a portion of garlic bread.

They leave a 10% tip.

How much do they pay altogether?

**B4**  Make up a multi-step problem of your own.

Paul has started a 'happy hour' when all the prices
on the board are reduced by 10%.

Groups of 10 or more people also get a further 20% off their total bill.

**C1**

5 people each have a main dish (choose what you think this would be).

They have 3 portions of garlic bread and 2 portions of coleslaw.

Record their bill and calculate the 10% reduction.

coleslaw 49p
garlic bread £1.12

**C2**

Chen and his 9 friends decide to eat during the 'happy hour'.

Choose their meals for them, work out their bill and calculate the reduction.

How much did they save?

**C3**

Ryan, Kat and Verity are too late for 'happy hour'.

They order a large seafood pasta, a regular meat feast pizza and a small vegetable
lasagne, plus garlic bread for 2.

How much more do they pay for their food by eating later?

| **Key idea** | It is often efficient to use standard written methods for solving money problems with several stages. |
|---|---|

# SP3.1 Which way to multiply?

| Key idea | A standard written method for multiplication is often, but not always, more efficient than mental methods. |
|---|---|

★1    Tins of coke cost 19p each and are packed in boxes of 12.

How much does a box cost?

★2    Bottles of coke cost 21p and are packed in crates of 18.

    **a**    How much does 1 crate cost?

    **b**    How much do 4 crates cost?

A1    Zenab buys fruit for her shop.

Kiwi fruit cost 17p each and are packed in trays of 16.

    **a**    How much does Zenab pay for 2 trays of kiwi fruit?

    **b**    How much does she pay for 8 trays of kiwi fruit?

A2    Zenab looks at mangoes for 45p each.

How much would 29 mangoes cost?

A3    She notices a special offer on mangoes. A bag of 12 mangoes costs just £4.

Figs cost 18p each and are packed in trays of 24.

Zenab buys a tray of figs and a bag of mangoes.

How much does she spend altogether?

**B1** Look at the market stall on page 101.

Pineapples are good value as well.

Small, single pineapples cost 65p each, but a bag of 20 costs only £12.

What is the least that Zenab could pay for 36 pineapples?

**B2** Figs cost 18p each and are packed in trays of 24.

If Zenab has a total of £25 to spend and has already bought 2 bags of pineapples, how many figs can she afford to buy?

**B3** Zenab sells figs for 25p each. How much profit could she make by selling 3 trays of figs?

**B4** Make up 2 more multi-step problems about Zenab and her shop.

**C1**

Joely has £6 to spend.

Today pineapples cost 75p each and figs are 3 for 50p.

**a** What different combinations of figs and pineapples can she buy?

**b** What if ... kiwi fruit are on offer as well at 2 for 25p?

What different combinations of figs, pineapples and kiwi fruit can she buy?

**C2** Paul has a budget of £30. He needs an equal number of figs, pineapple and kiwi fruit.

**a** Find the greatest number of each he can buy and what money he has left.

**b** What if he needs only half as many pineapples as each of the other kinds of fruit?

| **Key idea** | A standard written method for multiplication is often, but not always, more efficient than mental methods. |

# SP3.2 Which way to divide?

| Key idea | Whichever way you choose to divide to solve a problem, you are using your knowledge of inverses and interpreting remainders. |
|---|---|

★1    **a**    30 children can use the swimming pool for each half hour lesson.

         How many lessons are needed for 215 children?

*Count in 30s.*

   **b**    If 2 more children could swim each lesson, how many lessons would be needed?

★2    How many 30 cm lengths of wood can be cut from a 215 cm length?

*Round up or down?*

**A1**    There are 14 chocolate bars in a bag.

How many bags should I buy for 153 children to have a chocolate bar each?

**A2**    A minibus holds 15 passengers plus the driver.

How many minibuses are needed to take 162 children to the skate park?

**A3**    25 apples are packed in each box.

How many boxes are needed to pack 1410 apples?

**A4**    Stephen has £2.52.

   **a**    How many coloured pencils could he buy at 22p each?

   **b**    He thinks he could buy 6 gel pens instead. How much is a gel pen?

**B1** Shireeka wants to buy 18 matching envelopes for her party invitations.

There are 2 types of envelope in the local shop:
the cheaper ones cost 13p each and the smarter ones cost 17p each.

She has £2.90. Which type of envelope can she afford?

Round up or down?

**B2** Jack has been given 411 bulbs to plant in the large tub outside the school.

**a** How many tubs can he fill if he puts 22 in each one?

**b** How many more bulbs does he need to fill one more tub?

**B3** Gilly bought 15 tickets for the local theatre.

Some cost £4.80 and the rest cost £5.30 each.

The bill was £72.50.

Which tickets did she buy?

**B4** Each row in the cinema holds 22 people, and 21 rows are still empty.

576 people are in the queue outside.

How many of them won't get a seat?

**C1** Which two numbers multiply together to give 4032?

Check your solutions by using the inverse operation.

There is more than one solution!

**C2** Which two consecutive whole numbers multiply together to give 4692?

Write down a strategy for finding the solution.

**C3** Make up similar problems of your own for your partner to solve.

| Key idea | Whichever way you choose to divide to solve a problem, you are using your knowledge of inverses and interpreting remainders. |
|---|---|

# SP3.3 Using metric and imperial units

| Key idea | You can convert imperial units into metric units using multiplication or division. |
|---|---|

**A1** A jug measures in pints or millilitres.

1 pint is about ☐ millilitres.

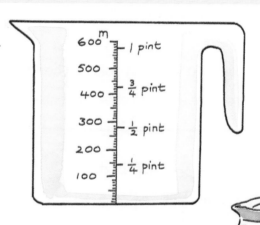

**A2** The jug holds 2 pints of milk.

**a** How many litres does it hold?

**b** How many times can I fill it from a 4-litre carton of milk?

**A3**

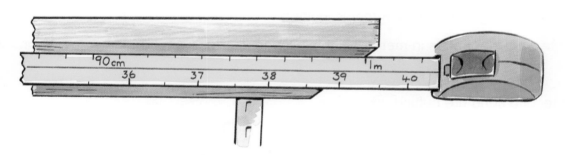

**a** The shelf is 1 metre long.

About ☐ inches make a metre.

**b** A length of 12 inches is called 1 foot and a length of 3 feet is called 1 yard.

| | | | | |
|---|---|---|---|---|
| 12 inches (in) | = | 1 foot (ft) | | |
| 24 in | = | 2 ft | | |
| ☐ in | = | 3 ft | = | 1 yard (yd) |
| ☐ in | = | 6 ft | = | 2 yd |

**c** Copy and complete the table.

| 1 metre | just over 3 feet |
|---|---|
| 2 metres | |
| 4 metres | |
| 10 metres | about 33 feet |

**A4**

Brenda is doing a 10 km run.

Her dad asks her how many miles that is.

> 1 mile is about 1600 m.

**a** Write down the calculation that is needed to answer his question.

**b** Work out the answer.

**B1**

Sinead is making a wedding cake for her cousin from an old recipe.

She has most of the ingredients, but still needs these.

8 ounces of butter
12 ounces of raisins
1 lb of currants

> 1 pound (lb) = 16 ounces (oz)
> 1 oz is about 28 g.

The shop only sells things in metric weights.

Write what she needs in metric weights. Round your answers to the nearest 10 grams.

**B2** Janet and Jana are putting up a fence.

> 1 metre is about 3 feet.

Their garden is 90 feet long and 25 feet wide.

About how many metres of fencing will they need to go round both the long sides and the end of the garden?

**B3**

Peter has made 2 gallons of blackcurrant cordial for the school fete.

1 gallon = 8 pints
1 pint is about 570 ml.

He puts it into 250 ml and 500 ml bottles.

How many of each can he fill?

You can choose the combinations of bottles that you use.

**B4**

Marika's gran has given her some recipes, but all the ingredients are given in imperial units.

Convert them into metric units for Marika.

1 teaspoon = 5 ml
1 tablespoon = 4 teaspoons
1 ounce = 28 grams

*Honey Bread*
1lb of honey
12 ounces of flour
2 ounces of sugar
1 teaspoon of baking soda
rind of 1 lemon
2 eggs
cinnamon
2 ounces of walnuts

*Granny's Cake*
5 ounces of butter
6 ounces of sugar
7 ounces of flour
$1\frac{1}{2}$ teaspoons of baking soda
1 tablespoon of milk
3 eggs
Filling:
8 ounces of jam
$\frac{1}{2}$ pint of cream

**C1**

Seema's car does 35 miles to the gallon.

1 mile is about
1.6 km.

**a** If she travels 196 km, how many gallons of petrol will she need for the journey?

**b** She finds she can only buy petrol in litres.

How many litres will she need for her journey?

**C2**

Write a similar problem of your own that involves conversion from metric units to imperial ones and imperial units to metric ones. Work it out!

| **Key idea** | You can convert imperial units into metric units using multiplication or division. |
|---|---|

# SP3.4 Calculators and rounding

| Key idea | Be careful how you use rounding when you are solving problems. |
|---|---|

You need a calculator. Use it only when you need to.

**★1** Round these amounts to the nearest euro.

[a] 11.1 euros     [b] 19.7 euros     [c] 39.4 euros     [d] 99.5 euros

**A1** Aisha and Rula are going to France. They change their pounds in the travel shop. The exchange rate is 1.6 euros for each pound.

To the nearest whole number, how many euros would they get for

[a] £10?     [b] £20?     [c] £5?     [d] £85?     [e] £126?

**A2** Darius and Joe are going to Austria. They need schillings for their pounds. The exchange rate is 21.51 schillings to the pound.

To the nearest whole number, how many schillings do they get for

[a] £100?     [b] £150?     [c] £175?     [d] £349?     [e] £606?

**A3** Aisha and Rula each buy a coffee to take away. There is no VAT charged. Darius and Joe have coffee in the shop so they have to pay VAT.

How much VAT is due on a cup of coffee that costs £1.20 if it is charged at

[a] 10%?     [b] 20%?     [c] 15%?     [d] 17.5%?

**B1** Repeat A3 for a cup of hot chocolate that costs £1.35.

If you use a calculator, write down an approximate answer first.

Give your answers to the nearest penny.

**B2** Sarah and Seb are checking exchange rates at the travel shop.

| | | | | | |
|---|---|---|---|---|---|
| | Australia (dollar) | 2.53 | | Japan (yen) | 170.36 |
| | Austria (schilling) | 21.51 | | Norway (krone) | 12.82 |
| | Canada (dollar) | 2.02 | | USA (dollar) | 1.37 |

**a** Sarah's weekend at a hotel in Austria costs 3227 schillings.

How much is this to the nearest pound?

**b** Sarah's sister is going to Australia.

How many Australian dollars will she get for £850?

**c** Seb thinks that a Canadian dollar is worth more than a US dollar. Sarah disagrees.

Who is right? Explain your answer.

**d** Seb's friend tells him that a cup of coffee costs 204 yen in Japan. He thinks that is very expensive.

Write a sentence to explain why it is not.

**e** Sarah discovers that a sports top will cost her

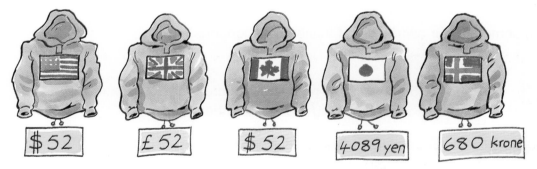

$52     £52     $52     4089 yen     680 krone

In which country is the top cheapest? Explain your reasoning.

You need an up-to-date list of exchange rates and a catalogue or price list.

**C1** Work out the cost of items in foreign currencies and euros.

**C2** Use the catalogue or price list to make up some questions of your own.

| Key idea | Be careful how you use rounding when you are solving problems. |
|---|---|

# SP3.5 Investigating a general statement

> **Key idea** | Find examples to match a general statement to help explain it.

### ★1

You need a calculator.

$$3 \times 3 = 9 \qquad 8 \times 8 = 64 \qquad 11 \times 11 = 121$$

[a] Find all the square numbers between 1 and 150.

[b] Explain how you know that you have found them all.

### A1

Investigate and explain this statement.

> For any 3 consecutive numbers, the product of the end
> numbers is less than the square of the middle number.

**Example**

4, 5, 6 are three consecutive numbers.

- the square of the middle number is $5 \times 5 = 25$
- the product of the end numbers is $4 \times 6 = 24$
- 24 is 1 less than 25, so the statement is true for 4, 5, 6

Try some of your own to see if this always happens.

> Use tables to help organise your working and diagrams to help with the explanation.

### B1

> If you take 5 consecutive numbers, square the middle number
> and multiply the end numbers, ...

**Example**

Take 3, 4, 5, 6, 7

- square 5
- multiply $3 \times 7$

[a] What do you notice? Try some more examples.

[b] Can you make a general statement about your results?

[c] Can you explain why this happens?

**B2**

Look back at B1.

Follow the same steps for 7 consecutive numbers and 9 consecutive numbers.

**a** Make general statements for 7 consecutive numbers and 9 consecutive numbers.

**b** Try to make a general statement about all your results.

**c** Can you explain why this happens?

> Use tables to help organise your working and diagrams to help with the explanation.

**C1**

**a** Write a pair of numbers.

**6  8**

Now re-write the pair of numbers so that one number is 1 less than before and the other is 1 more than before.

**5  9**

Find the product of both pairs of numbers.

**6 x 8  and  5 x 9**

Record your results.

**b** Try this with other pairs of numbers that are related in the same way.

What happens?

**c** Make a general statement about your findings and try to explain why it is always true.

> Look at differences between the numbers and between the products.

**C2**

Explore mathematical reference books, computer programs or web sites to investigate and record other interesting general statements about numbers.

| Key idea | Find examples to match a general statement to help explain it. |

# Basic skills with a calculator

> **Key idea** Before using a calculator you should have an approximate idea of the answer. After using a calculator you should choose a way to check the answer.

You need a calculator.

**A1**    a   127 + 496 = ☐          b   5623 − 4877 = ☐

           c   498 × 45 = ☐          d   7072 ÷ 68 = ☐

**A2**    Check your answers for A1.

           Write down how you did it.

**B1**    Solve these problems. Show how you checked each answer.

           a   Multiply 37 × 29.

           b   Find the difference between 6218 and 8156.

           c   Find the sum of 769, 972 and 615.

           d   Divide 4104 by 24.

**B2**    a   What is the total of your 4 answers in B1?

           b   Turn your calculator upside down to discover the name of the girl at the top of the page.

**B3**  Sam is in charge of the school stationery shop today.

a  Amie buys a ruler, an angle measurer and a pen.

How much does she pay altogether?

b  Phil buys a notepad, an eraser and a pack of colouring pencils.

How much does he pay?

c  Mrs Watts buys 6 pairs of compasses. What does this cost?

d  Mr Adams buys 8 of one item. He pays £11.20. Which item did he buy?

e  The secretary buys 24 pencils and pays with a £5 note.

What change must Sam find?

f  Imagine you have a £5 voucher to spend in the shop.

What would you buy?
Make a list. You would want to use as much of the voucher as possible.

| **Key idea** | Before using a calculator you should have an approximate idea of the answer. After using a calculator you should choose a way to check the answer. |
| --- | --- |

# Think about what answer to expect

| Key idea | Think about what answer to expect before using your calculator. |
|---|---|

**A1**  Use the constant function to find the missing numbers.

  **a**  16, 12, 8, 4, _____, _____, _____, _____

  **b**  47, 27, 7, −13, _____, _____, _____, _____

  **c**  −9, −5, −1, 3, _____, _____, _____, _____

  **d**  3, 9, 27, 81, _____, _____, _____, _____

> Try to predict the answers.

**A2**  **a**  Liam sets the constant function to divide by 3.

  He enters 18 and presses ⬚= 3 times.

  Write down the numbers displayed.

  **b**  Write 0.6666666 as a fraction.

  **c**  Lucy sets the constant function to divide by 6.

  She enters 72 and presses ⬚= 3 times.

  Write down the numbers displayed.

  **d**  Write 0.3333333 as a fraction.

**A3**  Lucy chooses one red number and one green number.

**6**   **4**        **6**   **18**

   **2**        **9**

She divides her red number by her green number.

  **a**  Which numbers give an answer of point 3 recurring?

  **b**  Which numbers give an answer of point 6 recurring?

**B1**

**Grange Castle**
Entry prices
Adults £2.40
Children free

4356 adults have bought tickets this season.

How much money has been collected?

**B2**

3192 copies of the guide booklet have been sold
and a total of £3032.40 has been paid.

How much does each guide booklet cost?

**B3**

The shop needs to make £100 from the sales of postcards.

How many must be sold?

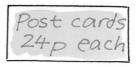

Post cards
24p each

**B4**

The keep on its mound is $2\frac{1}{2}$ times the height of the walls.

If the walls are 11.7 m high, how high is the keep?

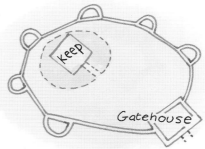

**B5**

This plan shows the keep as a square.

If the keep covers 324 m² of ground,
how long is each side of the square?

| **Key idea** | Think about what answer to expect before using your calculator. |

Using the memory to solve problems

| Key idea | Use the calculator's memory to store the answer to part of a problem. |

You need a calculator.

★1 Imagine the ⊞ key on your calculator is broken, and you cannot use it.

Instead use M+ and MR (recall memory) to find the total cost of

a    a dictionary and a pencil case

b    a set of pens and a file

c    a dictionary and a notebook

d    a pencil case and a file

e    all 5 items

Record your working.

**A1** For each of the following find the total cost and the change from £20.

Use the memory in your calculator to help.

**a** a notebook and a set of pens

**b** a calculator and a file

**c** a sketchbook and a pencil case

**d** a sketchbook, a set of pens and a calculator

**e** a file, a dictionary, a pencil case and a notebook

**B1**  Find the answers and record the key sequence.

a  $(57 \times 8) + (26 \times 9)$

b  $(49 \div 2) + (83 \div 4)$

c  $(23 \times 48) - (17 \times 63)$

**B2**  A special meal has been organised for the village outing.

a  One group orders
5 pizzas and 4 apple pies.

What is the total cost?

b  Another group orders
2 roast chicken meals,
1 pizza and 3 apple pies.

What is their change
from £20?

c  The total bill for a third
group comes to £37.50.

They ordered 3 pizzas,
4 roast chicken meals
and several ice creams.

How many ice creams
were ordered?

*Village Outing*

• *Pizza*          £4.65
• *Roast*
  *Chicken*      £4.95
• *Apple pie*     £1.30
• *Ice cream*      75p

## Master the maze

There is only one safe route through this maze.

Collect points as you go.

| 80 | 87 | 91 | 25 |
| --- | --- | --- | --- |
| 1312 ÷ 16 | 11·5 × 8 | 7·6 × 3·5 | 12342 ÷ 56 |
| 82 | 33 | 96 | 218 |
| 2541 ÷ 77 | 80 × 1·2 | 72 × 0·5 | 806 ÷ 6 |
| 215 | 98 | 36 | 127 |
| 332 × 0·8 | 1848 ÷ 66 | 140 × 0·7 | 2·1 × 35 |
| 266 | 28 | 252 | 74 |
| 395 ÷ 15 | 1134 ÷ 4·5 | | 144 ÷ 1·4 |

- Enter the maze and put a counter on the first square.

- Enter the number in red into your calculator's memory.

- Carry out the calculation in green. The answer tells you which square to go to next.

- Put the counter on this square.

- Add the number in red to the number already stored in the memory.
  This is your score so far.
  Complete the calculation in green to find where to go next.

- Continue moving through the maze, adding to your score.

- At the exit, pause to find your total score.
  Turn your calculator upside down to learn the name of the beast.

| Key idea | Use the calculator's memory to store the answer to part of a problem. |
| --- | --- |